Stock Investing for Students

A Plan to Get Rich Slowly and Retire Young
(Educating our youth to financial independence)

By Alan Ellman: The Blue Collar Investor

Tax Chapter by Owen Sargent, CPA

Stock Investing for Students

Second Printing: January 2014

ISBN: 978-1-937183-92-9

Printed in the United States of America
Published by Digital Publishing of Florida, Inc.
www.digitaldata-corp.com

"Success depends upon previous preparation, and without such preparation there is sure to be failure"

Confucius

Table of Contents

Appendix

Foreword

Our high schools and colleges are failing to prepare young people to successfully manage their financial futures. For this reason, I have been committed to teaching college students how to manage risk in the stock market for the past seven years. I personally know how many thirst for this type of education and the gap that this book fills. I have had to draw from over 40 years of investment experience and countless stock market "how-to" books to prepare the most effective materials for my students. Now, in this new book, Alan Ellman has made my task a lot easier. With *Stock Investing for Students*, Dr. Ellman has managed to provide – in a manner that even the most novice of investors will find easy to understand - all of the critical information students need to begin paving the path toward a secure financial future through sound investing. I cannot wait until I can assign this book as mandatory reading for all of my students!

This book is truly unique. It was specifically written to provide young people with a practical rule-based plan for achieving financial success in the stock market, though us older folks will find it plenty useful as well. Given that this book was written specifically for students, Dr. Ellman's strategy is appropriate for the cash-strapped novice, however those who have more robust savings to invest will find it equally useful. Unlike the majority of today's financial literature, this book is not filled with theory and financial jargon; rather, it provides the practical information needed to succeed in the stock market, and a realistic plan on how to utilize that information to generate consistent returns over time. The book assumes no knowledge of financial terms, and each chapter includes a set of definitions to make the material easy to understand.

I especially like the book's handling of the concepts of investing versus trading. Dr. Ellman embraces the investor's approach of holding onto winning stocks for the longer term, but also utilizes the trader's more nimble approach to minimize losses, as he shows us how to prevent small losses from growing into large losses while holding onto our gains.

This book does not overwhelm the reader with ponderous financial information. Instead, the information presented forms the basis of a set of rules that are introduced in each chapter. For example, Chapter Two explains concepts such as a company's capitalization and PE ratio, and uses these characteristics to establish criteria for selecting stocks. Similarly, Chapter Three educates the reader about some of my favorite technical tools, and demonstrates, for example, how to use these indicators to evaluate stocks and enter and exit stock positions. By the way, all of these rules and the full game plan are summarized in a nice format in Appendix IV and V.

Unlike many stock market books, which try to entice the reader into purchasing the author's software or stock selection service, this book shows the reader how to use free internet based services for screening stocks and creating stock charts. Dr. Ellman shows us how to interact with these websites to use the rules that he teaches, a particularly nice feature of his book which alone justifies its price.

The book is crammed with practical information, from selecting a broker and placing orders, to setting up a stock watch-list, to diversifying one's portfolio. It has the best comparison of the pros and cons of mutual funds and Exchange Traded Funds

(ETFs) that I have ever seen. Chapter 9, written by a tax expert, introduces both novice and experienced investors alike with the ins and outs of the tax implications on profits and losses. I especially like this chapter's discussion of Roth Individual Retirement Accounts (IRAs), which I urge all of my students to open.

I could go on and on about the benefits to be obtained from reading this book. But the most important to me is that Dr. Ellman has "walked the talk." He has successfully taught himself to invest in stocks, and has spent much of his time educating people how to profitably write covered call options, an advanced topic introduced in Chapter 12, and the subject of three of his prior successful books.

In sum, this is the most important stock market primer I have had the privilege to read. I believe it will make a difference to the future financial welfare of many people, young and old. I wish I had written it!

Eric D. Wish, Ph.D.
Worden, Sir Silent Knight,
And author,
WishingWealthblog.com

July, 2013

Acknowledgments

This is the fourth book I've written in a six-year period. As was the case with my prior publications, my journey was a long and arduous one but I loved every minute of it, in large part due to the understanding, emotional support and love I received from my family:

My Mom, Minnie: who continues to give me way more credit than I deserve.

My son Jared and my daughter (in-law) Aubrey: who gave me my first grandson.

My son Craig: Who edited this book like no one else can.

My stepson David: who, like me, is enjoying the excitement of a new career.

My grandson Seneca: who is the new light of my life.

Barry Bergman: an adopted family member who offered invaluable feedback enhancing the quality of the finished product.

My beautiful wife, Linda: who only offered love and support when I sat typing in front of my computer after promising to sit with her to watch a movie.

Your love and support will never be taken for granted and I will work very hard to let you know how much I appreciate all you've given to me. Now, Linda, let's go watch that movie!

Special thanks to Dr. Brian S. Brooks, Professor Emeritus, Missouri School of Journalism, whose popular lectures are always filled to capacity with promising writers, as is evidenced by the photo of his classroom featured on the cover. We are grateful for your permission to use this image, and for your gift of higher education, every day. You can reach Dr. Brooks at: BrooksBS@missouri.edu

Barbara Karnes: For sharing her unique skills and creating the outstanding artwork for the book covers.

Dr. Eric Wish: For writing such a well-crafted and generous foreword to this book.

Introduction

How would you like to retire a millionaire at a young age? No, this book is *not* another "get-rich-quick" scheme. Rather, it's a get rich in forty years *plan* in which you will learn how to construct your own wealth-building portfolio based on sound fundamental, technical and common sense economic principles. An investment portfolio can consist of four major asset classes: stocks, bonds, fixed income vehicles (such as money market funds and certificates of deposit) and real estate. This book will focus on the stock market because historically, stocks have outperformed the other asset classes, and also happen to be my favorite investment asset class.

When I was growing up, there was no education in our school system relating to the stock market or investing in general. Zero! During my earlier years, only the mere basics were taught - reading, writing, and arithmetic. As the years progressed, I experienced courses such as geometry, physics, and calculus to name a few. While these courses enhanced my knowledge and helped architect the person I am today, after graduating from dental school it became readily apparent that a huge hole existed in the fabric of my education. I was in massive debt and needed money to support my wife and first son, a precarious problem to say the least given that my income at the time was basically zero. Ironically, after living off of borrowed money to get through college and dental school, I began my professional career needing to take out yet another sizeable loan to build my dental practice. But I had so many questions. How do I obtain the financing I need? How do I balance a checkbook? After I start making money, how should I invest it, if at all? Unfortunately, these were questions that my 20 years of education left me woefully ill-equipped to answer. I was financially illiterate and forced to teach myself the hard way - by making mistakes and correcting them. It was all about trial and error. With this book, my hope is provide you the fundamentals of investing so that you can begin, at an *early* age, paving your own path towards financial independence without having to learn the hard way like I did.

As a student, there are so many forces pulling at you. The social pressures associated with things such as driving a car, making the team, getting a date for the big dance (and ensuring your parents don't embarrass you in front of your date for the big dance), can be overwhelming to say the least. And let's not forget trying to keep your grades up! With all of this pressure, your future as an adult with a family is likely one of the last things on your mind. Understandable. However, the irony here is that *now* this is the time in your life when you can take actions that impact your future in a more profound way than at any other time in your life. You, the student, have a unique advantage over every adult you know. This uncommon opportunity is one that only our youth possess, and it passes much too quickly. You have *time* on your side. I was oblivious to this opportunity when I was a student. I was too preoccupied with all of those social pressures and forces pulling at me, and while my studies were always a top priority, the high grades I received in calculus and biology fell far short of arming me with the financial literacy I desperately needed once I began working in "the real world." As a student, I had been staring at one of the greatest financial opportunities I would ever have – *time*. But I couldn't see it, and there wasn't anybody to show me that this tremendous opportunity existed, or to even inspire me to uncover its existence. I will not let the same thing happen to you.

For most adults, the idea of self-investing in the stock market is overwhelming, or at the least, intimidating. For students, this idea may seem inconceivable. I will debunk that myth and prove to you that it does not take a rocket scientist to become a successful stock market investor. Success, more than anything else, is a function of a solid financial education, a sound investment plan or strategy, and lots of motivation. To that end, let's make a deal right now: I'll provide you the education you need to become a successful stock market investor; in return, you provide the motivation. I will make every effort not to let you down if you promise to do the same for me. If we both hold up our ends of the agreement, we both win. You will retire at a young age with a secure financial future.

This book is written for you, the high school or college-age student. It is written in a way that I would have wanted a book to be written had I endeavored to learn the basics of stock market investing when I was your age. I have prepared all the information you need to begin self-investing in the stock market, including core guidelines you can utilize to construct a wealth-building portfolio tailored to your specific needs. Take your time digesting the information in this book. Plan on reading it twice. I will not talk down to you because we are now a team and you're my teammate. Besides, you are our future, and words can't describe how meaningful it would be for me to see you use the information provided in this book to ultimately achieve the financial freedom you seek. Most importantly, don't forget our pact - show me that motivation!

About This Book

I wrote this book with two primary goals in mind. First, I want to arm you with the educational background you need to successfully invest with stocks and other related financial instruments, such as mutual funds. However, a solid educational foundation, without a plan on how to actually utilize and implement this information, is not enough to succeed in the stock market. This brings me to my second primary goal – to provide you a simple, yet effective, *40-year investment game plan*, which you can start implementing *now*, as a student (i.e. age 18, but age and time frame can be adjusted). From time to time throughout this book, I will refer to this game plan as a "wealth-building" plan or portfolio, because that's exactly what it is – a plan that seeks to build wealth over time by maximizing profits and minimizing losses, and ultimately give you the opportunity to retire relatively young in a comfortable financial situation. This wealth-building plan consists of a set of rules that will assist you in choosing the best stocks for your portfolio, in addition to rules that will guide you in managing your positions (i.e. *when* to buy, sell, etc.). Each chapter in this book will emphasize the education, rules and guidelines necessary to successfully implement this wealth-building plan.

At the beginning of each chapter, a chapter outline, along with a section highlighting the chapter's wealth-building plan rules, will be provided. To reinforce these rules, they will be **bolded** in the body of the text and also summarized in the appendixes. As you read about these requirements, it may initially appear that a huge amount of time will be required to obtain the information you need, particularly with respect to the rules relating to stock selection. That is *not* the case. Our wealth-building plan was specifically created so that the majority of information needed can be obtained by plugging the rule-based criteria discussed throughout this book into free, automated stock screeners. These stock screeners allow you to simply (in the case of stock selection) plug in the relevant criteria, after which the screener will generate a list of stocks that meet our specified parameters (don't worry, this will make sense as you read through the chapters).

Please note that some of the chapters in this book - including the chapters on technical analysis and tax implications (Chapters 3 and 9) - will contain somewhat more advanced discussions of certain topics germane to that particular chapter. As your investment experience and knowledge grows, you may find some of these advanced discussions extremely useful, and ultimately may even decide to incorporate some of these ideas into your own personal investment strategy. That said, these advanced discussions are not necessarily critical for purposes of our wealth-building plan. But don't worry - I will specify which sections are necessary for our wealth-building plan, and which ones are for educational purposes only. Please remember that just because a particular discussion or section is not critical to our wealth-building plan, it does not mean you should automatically skip it. I strongly recommend that you read all such "advanced" sections that peak your interest. As the saying goes, knowledge is power, and I truly believe that there is no arena in which this saying is more applicable than the stock market arena.

Finally, keep in mind that our wealth-building plan begins with simple, safe investment vehicles such as mutual funds (baskets of stocks, as discussed later in this book), followed by individual stocks a few years down the road. Analysis of individual stocks can be mastered during the initial phase of our plan. Read this book for the first time to gain an overview of stock investing so that you can launch our game plan as early as possible. Then re-read the book several times so that you will have the ability to move into the second phase of our wealth-building plan (individual stocks) a few years from now.

Chapter 1

The Basics of Stock Investing

Chapter Outline

- Why invest in stocks?
- How much money do I need to start?
- Sources of income
- Investing vs. trading
- Types of risk
- Stock-related definitions
- Analysis-related definitions
- Management-related definitions
- Classifications of stock

Wealth-Building Rules in this Chapter

- Share price of $15 or higher
- Market-cap of $2 billion or greater
- Average daily trading volume of 500,000 shares per day or higher

To begin the process of building your successful financial future, you must first establish a sound fundamental, technical, and common sense investment foundation. Certain basic concepts and definitions should become second nature to you, and these concepts will be the focus of this chapter. Your goal for this first chapter is to *familiarize* yourself with these

1

concepts. As the book progresses, you will see these terms repeated and discussed in detail, and ultimately you will *master* the information. Whenever there is a rule or guideline that is essential in the construction of your student portfolio, that rule will be highlighted in **bold**.

Why Invest With Stocks?

Without an investment strategy that works, it is virtually impossible to earn more than we spend. For this reason, it is critical that we allocate a portion of our savings to make more money for us. Historically, stocks provide the highest potential returns over other asset classes, including bonds, savings accounts and real estate. It is not unreasonable to expect long-term stock investment to range between 8-10% annually, depending on the time frame calculated. *See appendix III for a long-term up-trending chart of the S&P 500, a widely used benchmark to evaluate how the overall stock market is performing.* **I will use the more conservative 8% figure as we move forward in this book.** This way, based on historical statistics, we have a minimum figure that should reasonably be achievable. It should be emphasized that investing in stocks is not without its risks. Short-term volatility (the amount of uncertainty or risk regarding price changes in a stock, mutual fund etc.) is one of the most notable of these risks. However, short-term volatility and other risks can be minimized by following a well-planned, intelligent long-term approach to stock investing, which is specifically what our wealth-building plan is all about!

I'm a Student: Can I Afford to Invest, and How Much Money Do I Need to Start?

You do not need to be earning a large income to start utilizing our wealth-building plan. More specifically, you will be asked to save $1,000.00 (to be discussed later in the book) to get started, and our plan will be based on the assumption that you earn an *average* income of $60,000 for the first 20 years of the plan, and $80,000 for the second twenty years. It is understood that, as a student, you will have a much lower income during your initial investment years than you will in your later years, so please do not worry. For a family with two income earners, each member will need to average slightly less than $700 per week in gross wages to adhere to the plan.

Sources of Income

The majority of people have two sources of income. The first source of income is called *active income*. Active income is income you earn for services performed, such as wages earned from a regular day (or night) job. *Passive income*, by contrast, is money that is earned with existing money (though there are varying definitions). For purposes of this book, income earned from investing in the stock market is considered passive income.

Most who do not have a career in finance simply don't realize how much additional passive income they can generate utilizing a successful stock investing strategy (including those who earn a modest active income). Of those that do realize these benefits, far too many begin actively investing when they reached their forties and fifties (like I did). Unfortunately, many of these individuals also *rely on brokers or financial advisors to make their investing decisions for them. Only a small fraction (if that) of the stock investing population are self-educated high school or college age students, or* otherwise began investing in stocks at a young age. This distinction is crucial, because with a rising long-term stock market and many years of investing, young investors such as yourself who invest wisely are almost certain to achieve impressive long-term returns (i.e. profits). My point here, and one that I will continue to make throughout this book, is that *time is money*; realizing at an early age the potential upside in utilizing your active income (some students hold part-time jobs while in school to generate a small active income) to generate passive income is the first step towards your goal of retiring with financial security at a relatively young age.

Investing vs. Trading

Investing implies taking a longer-term position in an equity (e.g. stock). Investors look to profit later on down the road, and are typically associated with "buy and hold" strategies. *Traders*, on the other hand, hold their positions for a *shorter* period of time, usually anywhere from a few hours to a few weeks. Traders enter (buy) and exit (sell) their stock positions much more frequently than investors, seeking to generate short-term profits. Given that an investment strategy requires less activity (fewer buy/sell transactions) than a trading strategy, investors typically pay less in commission fees, spend less time managing their positions, and enjoy lower levels of stress than traders. In fact, over time, investing has proven to be the more successful strategy of the two. That said, trading *can* be a more successful strategy than investing, particularly in the short term. In addition, given its fast-paced nature and the significant time requirements involved, trading also has the potential to build more discipline than investing. The philosophies championed in this book embrace *both* approaches. In particular, we will learn to enter our positions (buy our stocks) with the mindset of an investor, but will react to losing positions (positions that are losing money) with the mindset of a trader. This hybrid approach should bring us the best of both worlds - our chances for success will be high, our stress levels will be low, and we will learn the discipline that is crucial to successfully complete our journey to financial freedom.

Types of Risk

Generating income in the stock market is largely contingent upon establishing, and adhering to, sound fundamental, technical and common sense principles. However, the simple fact remains that when we make money in the stock market, we are effectively being paid for the *risk* we incurred when we made our initial investment. A risk-free investment such as U.S. Treasuries (fixed interest bonds backed by the U.S. government) ensures capital preservation (protects the initial investment) but generates low returns, which at times can actually be lower than the rate of inflation. Higher-risk investments, such as an investment in a biotechnology stock, have the potential to generate higher returns than a lower-risk investment, but are also more likely to result in a loss. We must be exposed to *some* risk to achieve our goal of retiring a financially secure at a relatively young age. To that end, it is crucial to understand that we can *control*, to a large degree, the types of risk we are exposed to and amount of risk exposure our investments face. The point here is that *risk management* is a crucial part of any successful investment strategy, including ours. Our strategy will seek to take "reasonable" risks and ultimately get paid very well for assuming those risks. Below is a summary of the main risks we incur when investing in the stock market:

- *Emotional Risk* - Logic and discipline can be negated by fear and greed

- *Inflation Risk* - If the costs of living increases more than our investment profits, our goals will not be met.

- *Interest Rate Risk* - Rising interest rates have a negative impact on the price of our stocks

- *Market Risk* - The price of our stocks may decline due to economic factors or other events that impact the overall market

- *Tax Risk* – When we sell an investment, such as a stock we own, for a profit (also known as "realizing" a profit), we get taxed on that profit. This tax is known as a *capital gains tax*. The capital gains tax levied on the sale of our investment profits is not necessarily always going to be the same. We will address the issue of minimizing the extent to which capital gains taxes eat into our investment profits in Chapter 9

In this book, we will learn to minimize the impact that these risks have on our level of investment success by adhering to a disciplined approach to investing, which stresses sound fundamental, technical and common sense principles.

Stock-Related Definitions

In the next three sections, we will be reviewing terms that we will subdivide into three categories: stock-related (descriptive terms), analysis-related (how we analyze our investment decisions) and management-related (terms we need to know after investments are made).

New investors should read through these terms carefully, however there is no need to memorize them. For now, simply familiarize yourself with these terms and refer back to this chapter as needed as you make your way through this book. In time, I assure you these terms will become part of your everyday investing vocabulary.

Average Daily Trading Volume (ADV) - The average number of shares of a particular security traded per day over a specified time period. ADV is a measure of the liquidity of a stock. Stocks with high ADVs can be easily traded and thus are considered more *liquid* than securities with lower ADVs. *Stocks with a high ADV are generally considered less risky, while stocks with a lower ADV are generally considered more risky.*

Bearish – Pessimistic investor sentiment that a particular security or market is headed downward. An investor who is "bearish on a stock" thinks that the price of that stock is going to go down.

Bond- A debt instrument issued for a period of more than one year with the purpose of raising capital by borrowing. The Federal government, states, cities, corporations, and many other types of institutions sell bonds. Generally, a bond is a promise to repay the principal along with interest (coupons) on a specified date (maturity).

Book Value – The total value of a company's assets that shareholders would theoretically receive if a company were liquidated.

Bullish – Optimistic investor sentiment that the price of a stock or overall market will rise. An investor who is "bullish on a stock" thinks that the price of that stock is going to go up.

Capital gain - An increase in the value of an investment that gives it a higher value than the purchase price. The gain is not realized until the asset is sold.

Consolidation – Sideways price movement of a stock where the forces of supply and demand are equal. There is no uptrend or downtrend.

Common Stock –Securities that entitle its holder to an equity ownership in the corporation, voting rights and a share of the company's success through dividends and/or capital appreciation. In the event a company goes bankrupt, a trustee is appointed to "liquidate" (sell) the company's assets. The money from the liquidation is used to pay off the company's debt, which may include debts to creditors and investors. Holders of common stock are at the *bottom* of the priority list to receive this money, behind bondholders, creditors, and preferred stock holders. The majority of the stock we will own will be common stock.

Dividend - A distribution of a portion of a company's earnings to its shareholders. The dividend is most often quoted in terms of the dollar amount each share receives (dividends per share). Dividends can also be quoted in terms of a percentage of the current market price, referred to as the *dividend yield*. The date you must have ownership of the shares in order to capture a dividend is known as the *ex-dividend date*.

Earnings from continuing operations – Earnings from those segments of a company's business that it considers to be normal, and expects to operate in for the foreseeable future.

Earnings per share – A company's total profit divided by the number of outstanding (owned by investors) shares.

Earnings Reports - Quarterly filings made by public companies to report their performance. These reports include items such as net income, earnings per share, earnings from continuing operations, and net sales. . Most companies file their earnings reports in the month following the end of each quarter (January, April, July, and October).

Equity - A stock or any other security representing an ownership interest. In this book, equity will apply to stocks and *securities* will apply to a broader category of stocks and exchange-traded funds.

Exchange-Traded Funds (ETFs) - Securities that track an index, commodity, or a basket of assets such as an index fund, but trade like a stock on a national securities exchange. ETFs are similar to mutual funds, however one major difference is that ETFs (unlike mutual funds) experience price changes throughout the day as they are bought and sold. See Chapter 5 for more details. An example would be QQQ which tracks the 100 largest non-financial companies on the NASDAQ Exchange.

Index - An imaginary portfolio (group of financial assets) of securities representing a particular market or a portion of a particular market. The S&P 500 is one of the world's most commonly used indexes.

Index Fund - A type of mutual fund (see definition for mutual fund below) with a portfolio constructed to mirror, or track, the components of a market index such as the S&P 500 Index. An index mutual fund is said to provide broad market exposure, low operating expenses and low portfolio turnover (Little buying and selling). *Indexing is a passive form of fund management that has historically outperformed most actively managed mutual funds.* We will consider utilizing index funds as one of our investment vehicles when formulating our "game plan" to wealth. Index funds are discussed in more detail in Chapter 5.

Industry - A classification that references a group of companies that are interrelated in their primary business activities. Some examples would include Oil & Gas, Tobacco, Construction Services and Metal Mining.

Initial Public Offering (IPO) - The first sale of stock by a private company to the public. Investments in IPOs are risky (just ask anyone who bought Facebook during its IPO on May 18, 2012) and will not be part of our game plan. Private companies "go public" usually in an effort to raise money and enhance prospects for a successful and expanding business.

Issue – The process of offering stocks or bonds to the public as a means of raising capital. This may be a first-time offering or in the form of additional shares.

Liquidity - The degree to which an asset or security such as stock or exchange-traded fund can be bought or sold in the market without affecting the security's price. Securities that can be easily bought or sold are known as liquid assets. Liquidity is characterized by a high level of trading activity-the higher the level of trading activity associated with a particular security, the more liquid that security is considered. For our wealth-building portfolio, **we will require our stocks to have a minimum average daily trading volume of 500,000 shares per day.** This will ensure a reasonable opportunity for favorable prices when executing trades and minimize the risk of market manipulation by unscrupulous traders.

Market Capitalization - The total dollar market value of all of a company's outstanding shares. Market capitalization is calculated by multiplying a company's shares outstanding by the current market price of one share. The investment community uses this figure to determine a company's size. Also referred to as "market cap."

Market Sectors - Groups of industries sharing common characteristics. Investors use market sectors to place stocks and other investments into categories such as technology, health care, energy, utilities and telecommunications. Each market sector has unique characteristics and a different risk profile.

Mutual Funds - An investment vehicle operated by money managers that is comprised of a pool of funds collected from many investors for the purpose of investing in securities such as stocks. Mutual funds attempt to produce capital gains and income for the fund's investors. A mutual fund's portfolio is structured and maintained to match the investment objectives stated in its *prospectus*. Some mutual funds are designed to track a particular index like the S&P 500. Mutual funds do not incur price changes during the day as do exchange-traded funds. We will be discussing mutual funds that mirror the S&P 500 and also the Total Stock Market. See Chapter 5 for more details on this topic.

National Securities Exchange - Usually referred to simply as "an exchange", a national securities exchange is a platform to sell securities to the investing public. The New York Stock Exchange and NASDAQ Exchange are two examples.

Net income - A company's total earnings (or profit). It is calculated by taking revenues and deducting the cost of doing business, depreciation, interest, taxes and other expenses.

Net sales - The amount of sales generated by a company after the deduction of returned items, allowances for damaged or missing goods and any discounts allowed.

Over-the-Counter (OTC) - Stocks that trade via a dealer (frequently over the phone) and don't trade on a national securities exchange such as NYSE. These are usually risky investments and will not be part of our wealth-building plan. Penny stocks (priced under $5) are examples of securities that trade over-the-counter.

Sector - An area of the economy in which businesses share the same or a related product or service. Sector is a much broader classification than is an industry (see market sector).For example, the Services Sector includes such industries as restaurants, retail drugs and schools among others.

Securities and Exchange Commission (SEC) - The federal agency whose primarily responsibility is administering and enforcing federal securities laws. When necessary, the SEC enforces securities laws through a variety of means, including fines, referral for criminal prosecution, and suspension of licenses, among others. Think of the SEC as the primary "stock cop" in the U.S.

Security – Financial instruments that represent financial ownership in a publicly traded company. They can be stocks, mutual funds or exchange-traded funds (ETFs). The securities we will deal with in this book are *equity* securities (as opposed to *debt* securities bonds).

Shareholder's equity - A firm's total assets minus its total liabilities. It represents the amount by which a company is financed through common and preferred shares.

Short Sale – The sale of a stock that is not owned by the seller, but rather borrowed from the broker. Short sellers expect the price of a stock to decline, but do not actually own the stock. They therefore borrow the stock (for a fee) from their broker, sell the borrowed stock (hoping the price goes down after the sale), and return the shares back to their broker by buying the stock back (also known as "closing the position"). A short-seller profits by buying the stock back at a price lower than the initial sale price, and loses money by buying the stock back at a price higher than the initial sale price. Short sales are risky transactions and not recommended in this book.

Standard and Poor's 500 (S&P 500) - An index consisting of 500 stocks selected by market size, liquidity and industry grouping, among other factors. The S&P 500 is designed to be a leading indicator of U.S. equities and is meant to reflect the risk/return characteristics of the large-cap universe. Many refer to the S&P 500 as "the market." Since it is made up of 500 of the most widely traded stocks in the U.S., it represents about 70% of the total value of U.S. stock markets. In general, the S&P 500 index gives a good indication of movement in the U.S. marketplace as a whole.

Stock – A type of security that implies ownership in a corporation and represents a claim on a portion of that company's assets and earnings. There are two types of stock:

common (the type we will deal with in this book) and preferred stock which has certain advantages and disadvantages which we will address later in this book.

Stock Split - A change in the number of shares outstanding (in circulation). The number of shares is adjusted by the split ratio, e.g. 2 to 1. For example, let's say you own 1,000 shares of stock XYZ, which has a current price of $10.00 The total cost of your investment in XYZ is thus $10,000 (1,000 shares x $10/share). In a "2 to 1 stock split," 1,000 shares of XYZ splits to 2,000 shares, but the current price of XYZ is cut in half to $5.00. After the 2 to 1 stock split, the total cost and current value of your investment in XYZ is still $10,000 (2,000 shares x $5/share), however the number of shares have increased (from 1,000 shares to 2,000 shares) and the *price per share* has decreased (from $10/share to $5/share). The lower price per share makes it less costly for small investors to own the stock. A *reverse stock split* (number of shares are reduced while the price per share is increased) is initiated by a company to make its price appear more impressive or to allow it to remain on an exchange that has a minimum per share price requirement. Chapter 8 contains a more fulsome discussion on stock splits.

Ticker Symbol – Also referred to as "the ticker," the ticker is an arrangement of characters (usually letters) representing a particular security that's listed on a national securities exchange or otherwise traded publicly. For example, Google's ticker symbol is "GOOG."

Volume - The number of shares or contracts traded in a security or an entire market (shares traded on the NYSE, for example) during a given period of time. Volume represents the amount of shares that trade hands from sellers to buyers as a measure of activity. For example, if buyer purchases 100 shares of stock from a seller, then the volume for that period increases by 100 shares based on that transaction. **As noted above, our wealth-building portfolios will contain stocks that have a minimum average daily trading volume of 500,000 shares per day.**

Analysis-Related Definitions

The following definitions relate to the stock selection process.

Beta - The amount a security moves in relation to movement of the market. A stock with a beta of "1" will move exactly with the overall market (S&P 500). Therefore, if the S&P 500 is up 4% in a year, a stock with a beta of "1" would be expected to also rise by 4% based on historical statistics.

CBOE Volatility Index (VIX) - A measure of the market's expectation of 30-day volatility. The VIX measures market risk, and is often referred to as the *investor fear gauge*.

Fundamental Analysis –A method of evaluating a company's stock by examining the company's main *financial statements* (the income statement and balance sheet). Thus, fundamental analysis focuses on things such as earnings, sales, debt, and equity. Fundamental analysis takes into consideration only those variables that are directly related to the company itself, rather than the overall health of the market. Unlike technical analysis (the second primary method of evaluating a company), fundamental analysis does not focus on a company's historical stock prices. Fundamental analysis is discussed in greater detail in Chapter 2.

Realize a profit – Locking in a profit by closing a position so that it is no longer exposed to risk.

Returns - The annual return on an investment expressed as a percentage of the total amount invested. Also called *rate of return*.

Technical Analysis – The second primary method of evaluating a company's stock, technical analysis attempts to predict future price movements of a stock by analyzing the historical price movements of that stock. Have you ever seen one of those so-called "experts" on T.V. discussing a stock by referring to a chart with a bunch of crazy lines all over it? If so, that expert was probably using technical analysis to evaluate the stock's potential growth. Technical analysts uses market data such as price charts, volume, and open interest to predict the future (usually short-term) behavior of a stock. Technical analysis assumes that market psychology influences trading in a way that allows price movements in a stock to be predicted. Technical analysis is discussed in greater detail in Chapter 3, where you will see that it's not nearly as complicated as Wall Street would like you to think!

Volatility - Refers to the fluctuation (*not* direction) of a stock's price. Volatility represents the deviation of day-to-day price changes in a stock, and measures the speed and magnitude at which a stock's price changes. Highly volatile stocks (large price swings) tend to be more risky, and many highly volatile stocks are associated with low trading volume, which makes them even riskier. We will avoid highly volatile stocks in our wealth-building portfolio.

Management-Related Definitions

These are terms that relate to management of our investment positions.

Diversification - A risk management technique that mixes a wide variety of investments within a portfolio. The rationale behind this technique contends that a portfolio of different kinds of investments will, on average, yield higher returns and pose lower risk than any individual investment found within the portfolio.

Dollar Cost Averaging - The technique of investing a fixed dollar amount on a regular schedule, regardless of the share price. Because the amount of money invested is fixed, dollar cost averaging ensures that more shares are purchased when prices are low, and that fewer shares are bought when prices are high. Thus, dollar-cost averaging lessens the risk of investing a large amount of money in a single investment at the wrong time.

Inflation - The rate at which the general level of prices for goods and services is rising, and, subsequently, purchasing power is falling.

Investment Retirement Plan (IRA) - A plan that individuals establish to prepare and plan for retirement. Usually, an IRA plan allows you to save money and defer taxes until you retire

Online Discount Broker - A stockbroker who carries out buy and sell orders online at reduced commissions but does not provide investment advice. TD Ameritrade and E*Trade are two examples.

Portfolio – A collection of financial assets such as stocks, mutual funds and ETFs owned by an investor.

Portfolio Management - The act or practice of determining the mix of assets held in a portfolio, and making investment decisions in connection with those assets in order to make the largest possible return. *Portfolio management requires organized lists of accurate information.* Portfolio management is discussed in further detail in Chapter 4.

Stop-Loss Trade Order - An order placed with your broker to sell a security when it reaches a certain price. There are several other market orders which will be discussed in Chapter 7.

Watch List - A list of securities that are in consideration for investment buy/sell decisions.

Classifications of Stock

We've all heard the terms, but do we really know what they mean? Small cap stocks, defensive stocks, cyclical stocks, income stocks, etc. Enough already, I'm getting a headache! These terms are bandied about on financial networks such as CNBC (one of the more popular cable television business news channels) like a tennis ball at Wimbledon. Getting to know these phrases and their potential impact on our portfolios is the objective of this segment.

Stocks are often classified into broad categories that have similar investment characteristics. Some are based on industry affiliations (for example, Apple Computer, Dell Computer and IBM are all part of the Computer Hardware industry), while others are based on the size of the particular company or other financial characteristics. Below is a list of several of the most important stock classifications that I feel is important for you to know and understand.

Market Capitalization Categories

Market Capitalization, or "market cap" as it's commonly referred to, categorizes a stock according to the value of all the company's outstanding *common* shares. To calculate a company's market cap, multiply the number of outstanding *common shares* by its current price. For example, if BCI Corp. has 1 million shares of outstanding common stock priced at $30 per share, its market cap is 30 million. The six main categories of market capitalization are summarized directly below. Bear in mind that the following monetary classifications are only approximations that may change over time, and that the following definitions may vary between brokerage houses:

- *Large-cap stocks* (over $5 billion) - This category is typically reserved for conservative "safety first" investors who favor steady (but modest) share appreciation over growth potential. Large-cap stocks are *usually* blue chip companies (see below) that have a large segment of market share, are extremely liquid and experience very little trading volatility.

- *Mid-cap stocks* ($1 billion to $5 billion) - Mid-cap companies are *usually* growth companies that are on their way to becoming large-cap, and perhaps blue-chip, stocks. Mid-cap stocks exhibit some of the safety that large- cap stocks do, but also retain some of the growth potential associated with small - cap stocks. In terms of a risk v reward analysis, many investors view mid-cap stocks as a healthy compromise between small and large-cap stocks.

- *Small-cap stocks* (less than $1 billion) - Small-cap companies are *usually* growth companies in the early stages of business that have aggressive marketing plans and high growth potential (*potential* being the operative word). Typically, these stocks are not as financially sound as larger, more established companies, and thus are considered riskier investments. Small-cap stocks also tend to be less liquid and more volatile than mid-cap and large-cap stocks.

- *Micro-cap stocks* ($50 million to $300 million) - Considered the riskiest of the market cap stock categories, micro-cap companies also tend to be fledgling growth companies of questionable financial stability. These stocks are typically illiquid and highly volatile, but also tend to the cheapest, and thus often offer the highest profit potential (*potential* again being the operative word).

- *Nano-cap* Under $50 million

Earlier in this chapter, we discussed how our wealth-building plan would seek to take "reasonable risks" that offer the highest potential rate of return. In my experience, mid-cap and large-cap stocks both exhibit a risk/reward profile that is in line with our goal. For this reason, **our wealth-building portfolio will contain mid and large-cap companies that have a market capitalization of at least $2 billion for our wealth-building portfolios.**

Blue-Chip Stocks

Blue-chip stocks are well-known, large cap companies. They have a reputation for great management and a history of profits and dividends. Blue-chip stocks trade on the NYSE, NASDAQ and other national securities exchanges. Examples include American Express, Coke and Disney.

Growth Stocks

Growth stocks represent companies whose sales and earnings are growing faster than the economy or a company's individual sector. Growth companies tend to reinvest a majority of their earnings into things such as research and development (R&D) to allow for further expansion, and therefore pay little or no dividends. Although some are considered riskier than other stocks, growth stocks offer greater potential for capital appreciation (an increase in stock price).

Income Stocks

Income stocks pay higher-than-average dividends to their shareholders. They are usually stable companies that have a large market share, and thus can afford to heavily reward their shareholders. Historically, public utility companies (e.g. American Electric Power Co., Inc.) have been considered income stocks. They are usually large-cap companies.

Defensive Stocks

These companies provide important goods and services that are used in all economic climates and thus tend to be stable all year around, even during a recession (a general slowdown in economic activity). Defensive stocks are typically associated with companies in the food, utilities, healthcare and non-durable goods (e.g. clothing, soap) industries. These stocks are less vulnerable to economic downturns, but perform below the market when the economy is strong. Examples of defensive stocks include Coca Cola and General Electric.

Cyclical Stocks

These are stocks whose prices tend to rise and fall with fluctuations in the general economy. They produce products that consumers tend *not* to buy during difficult economic times. The steel, automobile, and building materials industries tend to have stocks that trade cyclically. Note that *unlike* blue-chip stocks, cyclical stocks tend to cut (or eliminate) dividends during an economic downturn.

Emerging Growth Stocks

These companies are in the early stages of development. They are usually small or micro-cap companies with new products or services. Emerging growth stocks are extremely volatile and risky.

Penny Stocks

The term "penny stock" generally refers to a low-priced, speculative stock that sells for less than $5 per share. Penny stocks typically trade "over-the-counter" (OTC). They do not trade on a national securities exchange such as the Nasdaq or NYSE. Stay away! **We will favor equities that are priced $15 and higher for our wealth-building portfolios.** This will eliminate many lower-priced stocks that have low trading volume and can be easily manipulated by unscrupulous traders.

This is a receipt for shares of the stock of a foreign company that has been deposited in a U.S. bank. Its purpose is to facilitate trading in foreign securities in the United States. Investors can purchase shares in U.S. dollars and also receive dividends in U.S. dollars thereby eliminating the need to exchange currencies. It allows U.S. investors to diversify their portfolios internationally without having to use foreign markets.

Common Stock vs. Preferred Stock

We've all heard the terms common and preferred stock (or at least those of us who didn't skip the definitions listed in Chapter 1!). Are common shares only for retail, Blue Collar Investors like us, while the preferred shares are reserved for Wall Street insiders? Not exactly. Although both terms represent types of stock that may be issued by a corporation (as briefly highlighted in Chapter 1), several key differences exist which bear repeating here.

- *Common Stock* - A security that represents *ownership* in a corporation. It allows you to elect members of a Board of Directors and vote on corporate policy. This is the first type of stock a corporation will issue (before preferred stock). Not all corporations issue preferred stock. **We will be dealing only with common stock as we move forward in this book as these are the shares normally available to retail traders.** However, I will offer a brief definition of preferreds in the paragraph below.

- *Preferred Stock (also called "preferreds")* - A class of ownership in a corporation that has a higher claim on assets and earnings than common stock. Preferred

23

shareholders are usually entitled to dividend payments *before* common shareholders (that's us). Unlike common stock, preferred stock also contains characteristics of both debt (fixed dividends) and equity (appreciation potential). These shares are issued by companies that have already issued common shares, and typically appeal to investors who prefer income over capital appreciation (the same type of investors who may otherwise purchase bonds). The structure of preferred stock is specific to each corporation.

Summary

Descriptive Rules for Our Wealth-Building Portfolio

These rules apply to the type and characteristics of companies we will demand for our wealth-building portfolio. When we discuss our stock screener for analyzing and locating investment candidates, the term descriptive will be one of the categories available.

Please keep in mind that we will initiate our plan with broad market mutual funds or exchange-traded funds until a certain financial threshold is reached. The stock screening process will begin in a few years when we progress into individual stocks. Below are the initial descriptive screening rules when we arrive at the stock portion of our plan.

With literally thousands of stocks to choose from, we have already established an initial set of descriptive requirements or rules that we will use to "screen," or significantly narrow down, this large universe of securities to a smaller subset more suitable for our wealth-building portfolio:

- We will require our stocks to have a share price of $15 or higher

- We will only invest in companies that have a market-cap of $2 billion or greater

- We will only invest in securities that have an average daily trading volume of 500,000 shares per day or higher

Note that all securities that meet our descriptive requirements (i.e. pass this first set of screens) are *still only candidates* for our wealth-building portfolio. That's because these requirements *are only the beginning* of our security screening and selection process. We want securities that are the best of the best – ones that satisfy our risk tolerance and exhibit just the right combination of safety and "reasonable risk." Therefore, as we will learn in the chapters to come, *additional* requirements and screens must be applied to any security that is ultimately bestowed the honor of being selected for our wealth-building portfolio! And if you're beginning to think utilizing multiple rule sets for this screening process will become cumbersome and complicated, don't. In the next Chapter, we will see just how easy it is to use our free stock screeners that will do all the work for us!

Chapter 2

Fundamental Analysis –
The Power of the Financial Statements

Chapter Outline

- Overview of fundamental analysis
- The major financial statements
- Ratio valuation
- Summary of wealth-building portfolio rule requirements
- Introduction to online stock screeners

Wealth-Building Rules in this Chapter

- PEG ratios of "2" or less
- ROE of 15% or higher
- Positive EPS growth during the past 5 years
- Projected EPS growth of 10% or greater over the next 5 years
- Positive sales growth rate over the past 5 years
- P/B Ratios of "4" or less

Overview of Fundamental Analysis

In chapter 1, we learned the first step in the stock portion of our plan to get rich slowly and retire young – using several key descriptive rule requirements to screen for securities best suited for our wealth-building portfolio. The next step in this process applies a second set of screens using *fundamental analysis*. Fundamental analysis is a method of evaluating a company's stock by examining its *financial statements* (including measures such as earnings, sales and debt), and also involves analyzing industry conditions and the overall economy. The most important part of fundamental analysis, however, involves evaluating the financial statements of a company, which are the medium by which a company publically discloses information concerning its financial performance.

Why is fundamental analysis important? Put simply, fundamental analysis is the foundation of solid investing. It gives us a look at a company's DNA, or the overall health of a company. For our wealth-building portfolio, we only want to invest in the stocks of financially sound companies – ones that will continue to grow, earn money, and profit over time. Fundamental analysis helps us find those companies, or in other words, helps us determine which companies have strong fundamentals (are financially healthy), and which ones have weak fundamentals (are in big trouble). Similarly, fundamental analysis also helps us gain a better understanding of whether the price of the stock is undervalued (a good buy) or overvalued (a rip-off) at the current market price. Below are just a few of the important questions fundamental analysis seeks to answer:

- Has the company been making profits consistently, and have those profits been growing or declining over time?
- Is the company holding its own relative to its competition?
- Is company in an industry that is growing or declining in importance to the overall economy?
- Can the company pay its bills?
- Is management trying to "cook the books"?

Does a company's fundamental soundness (or lack thereof) affect stock price? Absolutely. The stock prices of companies with strong fundamentals tend to go up over time, while fundamentally weak companies typically see their stock prices fall. Not surprisingly, institutional investors (mutual funds, hedge funds, banks and insurance companies), or the "big boys" as I sometimes call them, also favor fundamentally sound companies. We want to own stocks that the institutional investors favor because their buying power is the primary fuel for a major increase in the price of a stock. Put differently, institutional investors usually buy stock in large quantities given their vast financial resources, and when they do, supply and demand dictates the price of the stock they are buying will experience a nice increase. If we own a stock that becomes extremely popular with institutional investors, there's a good chance we will see a nice spike in its price (note that it is always best to own the stock *before* the institutional investors start buying). Likewise, when institutional investors start selling a stock that we own, it's usually a bad sign of things to come (note that it is always best to sell a stock you own *before* the institutional investors start selling heavily, or *as early as possible* thereafter).

Now that we have a general understanding of fundamental analysis, let's briefly discuss how the rest of this chapter will play out. First, we're going to review the major financial statements, which are the primary sources of information institutional investors use to fundamentally evaluate companies. For purposes of our wealth-building portfolio, *it is not essential to master the contents of these financial statements*, so feel free to move past this topic and onto the next one (Ratio Valuation) if you so choose. Next, as mentioned, we will learn how to use ratio valuation to compare and select stocks. Ratio valuation uses information from a company's financial statements to form mathematical ratios that provide statistics that give us a quick way to get an idea of whether a stock is undervalued or overvalued. We will learn the most suitable ratios to use for our wealth-building portfolio and the corresponding values we derive from those ratios, which will give us our second set of wealth-building portfolio rule requirements for the stock portion of our plan. After we learn our new fundamental requirements, we will quickly review *all* the wealth-building portfolio rule requirements we have learned thus far. Which will bring us to the last portion of this chapter, where we will learn how to use our portfolio rule requirements in conjunction with online stock screeners to create a list of stocks that meet our wealth-building portfolio criteria. Don't worry - this will all make sense by the time you are done with this chapter. I promise!

The Major Financial Statements

There are three major financial statements: (1) the Balance Sheet; (2) the Income Statement; and (3) the Statement of Cash Flows. All three statements can be found in the 10-Q and 10-K reports discussed below. Remember, although I recommend you at least familiarize yourself with these statements, feel free to skip to the next section (Ratio Valuation) if you so desire. Either way, I am confident that these financial statements will ultimately become part of your everyday investing vocabulary as your trading experience and knowledge grows!

Balance Sheet

The balance sheet represents a record of a company's assets, liabilities and equity at a particular point in time. It basically shows that a company has to pay for all the things it has (assets) by either borrowing money (liabilities) or raising money from shareholders by selling stock (shareholders' equity). In

30

other words, the balance sheet is a "snapshot" of a company's net worth *on a specified date*. Balance sheets must follow the following formula:

$$Assets = Liabilities + Shareholder\ Equity$$

Assets represent the resources that the business owns or controls at a given point in time, and include items such as cash, inventory, machinery and buildings. Liabilities represent debt, and include items such as accounts payable and wages payable. Equity represents the total value of money that the owners (including shareholders) have contributed to the business, including retained earnings (the profit made in previous years). The SEC requires public companies to publically file earnings report*s quarterly* (on a form called a 10-Q) and *annually* (on a form called a 10-K), as will be discussed shortly.

Income Statement

The income statement, also known as a "profit and loss statement," measures a company's performance over a specific time frame. It presents information about sales, expenses and profit generated from the company's operations *over a given period*.

Statement of Cash Flows

The statement of cash flows represents a record of a company's cash inflows and outflows *over a period of time*. Typically, a statement of cash flows focuses on the following cash-related activities:

- Operating Cash Flow (OCF): Cash generated from day-to-day business operations
- Cash from investing (CFI): Cash used for investing in assets, as well as the proceeds from the sale of other businesses, equipment or long-term assets
- Cash from financing (CFF): Cash paid or received from the issuing and borrowing of funds

10-K and 10-Q

In the United States, the Securities and Exchange Commission (SEC) requires all companies that are publicly traded on a national securities exchange to submit periodic filings detailing their financial activities, including the financial statements mentioned above. The 10-K and 10-Q are two of the most well-known filings, and can be found on the SEC's website: www.sec.gov/edgar.shtml. However, these filings can usually be found in a more reader-friendly format on the website of the particular company you are researching (check the "investor relations" link).

The 10-K is an *annual* filing that discloses a business's performance over the course of the fiscal year. A company's financial statements for the recent year (balance sheets, income statement and statement of cash flows) can be found in the 10-K, and the SEC requires these financial statements to be audited by an independent accountant before the 10-K is filed (the auditor's report is a key part of the 10-K). In addition to the financial statements for the most recent year, the 10-K also provides information relating to a company's historical financial data, along with information describing the operations of the business, including the number of employees, biographies of managerial personnel and future plans for growth, among others.

Businesses also release something called an "annual report," which some people also refer to as the 10-K. The annual report is essentially the 10-K professionally packaged. It includes much, but not all, of the same information that can be found on the 10-K.

The 10-Q filing is a smaller version of the 10-K. The 10-Q reports a company's performance *after each fiscal quarter.* Each year, three 10-Q filings are released, one for each of the first three quarters. There is no 10-Q for the fourth quarter because the 10-K filing is released during that time. Unlike the 10-K filing, the SEC does not require 10-Q filings to be audited.

Ratio Valuation

Ratio valuation uses *figures from the financial statements* to form financial ratios or mathematical calculations that help us gain an idea of a company's valuation (undervalued, overvalued, etc.) and financial performance. Using ratio valuation is a key component in selecting the best stocks for our wealth-building portfolios.

So what does ratio valuation actually do, and how can it help us? Let's start with a basic, non-investment related analogy to get our feet wet with this concept. If two NFL quarterbacks both threw 15 touchdowns last year, who's the better quarterback? Knowing that statistic only, which quarterback would you rather have on your fantasy football team? Not sure? Me neither. What if I told you quarterback A threw 15 interceptions last year, but quarterback B only threw 5 interceptions? Which quarterback would you rather have on our fantasy football team now? Seems to me B is now looking a lot better than A. What if B had a completion percentage of 60% while A had one of 45%? B is definitely looking more and more like our man! That's ratio valuation in a nutshell - by comparing *multiple* data points, individual statistics become much more meaningful.

Let's walk through one more example before we delve into the second set of rules for our wealth-building portfolio. Assume you are trying to decide whether to invest in Company A or Company B. You know that both companies had earnings (profits) of $1 million in 2012. Which company is the better investment? Tough to tell - we need more information. Now assume that in 2011, Company A had earnings totaling $500,000, while Company B had $2 million in earnings. Given this new information, Company A now appears to be the better investment choice because it saw its earnings *increased* 100% from 2011 through 2012, whereas Company B's earnings *decreased* by 50% over the same time period. Applying additional valuation ratios may either confirm or deny this initial sentiment. However, the important takeaway here is that, just as in the NFL example, utilizing ratios (in this case, growth rate) provided additional perspective on two companies that initially did not appear to be distinguishable from each other.

Ratios will give more meaning and perspective to data points in the financial statements. Below is a brief discussion of some of the most well-known valuation ratios which you will use in your stock selection process. Most of these ratios can be found in the "key statistics" link on the www.finance.yahoo.com site. However, there is no need to look these up individually as they will be part of our free stock screening process. Specific requirements will be based on the generally accepted statistics representing sound financial or healthy corporate finances.

Price to Earnings Ratio (P/E Ratio)

Years ago, investors, stockbrokers and financial advisors wanted to know the "P/E" of an equity (stock) before making a buy-decision. Back then, if someone recommended that you buy a particular stock, your first question likely would have been "What's the stock's P/E?"

The P/E ratio is a valuation ratio that compares the price of a stock to its per share earnings, and tells you how much you are paying for the current price of a stock for each dollar of a company's earnings (profit). For example, if you buy a stock with a P/E ratio of 10, that means you are willing to pay $10 for each dollar of the company's profit, or 10 times the earnings for one share of stock. A different way of looking at it is that it will take 10 years of the company's earnings at the current rate to add up to your original purchase price. *Investors use P/E ratios to assess whether a stock is overvalued, undervalued, or priced just right. Those that rely on this valuation ratio generally view a stock with a low P/E ratio as cheap (i.e. a "good buy") and expect its price to eventually rise, and view stocks with high P/E ratios as overvalued and more risky.* To ascertain whether a stock's P/E ratio is "low" or "high," investors compare the stock's current P/E ratio to its own past P/E ratio(s) and the P/E ratios of other companies in the same industry. Some also compare this ratio to the PE over the overall market or the S&P 500.

To calculate the P/E ratio of a particular stock, simply divide the current price of one share of stock (also known as Price per Share) by Earnings per Share:

P/E Ratio = Price per Share/Earnings per Share (EPS)

If the *previous* four quarters of earnings are used for this calculation, you have calculated the stock's *trailing P/E*. If the expected earnings (analyst consensus) for the next four quarters are used, you have calculated the stock's *forward P/E*. Longer average time frames can also be used to calculate PE ratios. For example, if a stock is priced at $30 per share and its anticipated earnings over the next 5 years averages out to $2 per share, it's PE ratio is 15 ($30/$2).

The problem I noticed when I started evaluating P/E ratios was that many of the companies with *high* P/Es back in the early 1990s were the ones that performed the *best*. Investors who automatically dismissed companies with high PE ratios would have missed out on a myriad of investment opportunities if they didn't also factor in earnings growth. These were the growth companies. Institutional investors were willing to pay *more* for these companies, driving up prices due to *expectations* that earnings would increase. Peter Lynch, one of the most successful and well-known investors of all time, addressed this issue in his book *One up on Wall Street* by stating "the P/E ratio of any company that's fairly priced will equal its *growth rate.*" He added, "every stock price carries with it a built-in growth assumption." In other words, if the P/E ratio equals a stock's growth rate, the stock is fairly priced *no matter what* the P/E is. Therefore, *evaluating a PE ratio with respect to its growth is a more useful tool than using the PE ratio by itself.* For example, if Company A is projected to have two times the earnings growth as Company B, investors will be willing to pay more for Company A. Thus, a P/E of 15 may be fairly priced for Company B, and a P/E of 30 may be fairly priced for Company A. Dividing by growth projections will put these two companies on a level playing field. Enter the *PEG ratio.*

Price/Earnings to Growth (PEG) Ratio

The PEG ratio is valuation ratio that is also used to determine the value of a stock (e.g. overpriced, underpriced, etc.) while accounting for the company's earnings growth. In other words, the PEG ratio (unlike the P/E ratio) accounts for how much the company will earn next year compared with what it earned this year. The PEG ratio is calculated as follows:

$$PEG = PE\ Ratio/Annual\ EPS\ Growth$$

The PEG ratio, like the P/E ratio, can be trailing or projected, and EPS growth can represent expected growth over the next year, or over the next five years. Like P/E ratios, a lower PEG ratio is also considered "better" (cheaper), and a higher PEG is generally considered "worse" (expensive). *A stock that is reasonably priced will have its PEG equal to 1 or lower.* The PEG ratio is not an exact, scientific number because it is based on *expected* growth. However, to completely ignore the PEG Ratio because it is subject to the limitations of projecting future events (expected growth) is *too conservative* a strategy for us – it would likely result in missed buying opportunities, especially for growth companies. Remember, we are willing to take "reasonable" risks, and relying on a company's expected growth (and consequently, the PEG ratio itself), in conjunction with our other fundamental and technical screens, is a reasonable risk for our investment purposes. Accordingly, we will use the PEG ratio as a screen to select stocks for our wealth-building portfolios. More specifically, **we will require our stocks to have PEG ratios of "2" or less.**

Back to our football analogy. If two running backs both gained 1,000 yards last year, but running back A has shown declining stats the past few years, while running back B has boasted accelerating stats, wouldn't we be willing to pay B more than A? That's our football PEG ratio!

Return On Equity (ROE)

ROE is the amount of a company's net income returned as a percentage of shareholder equity. It measures a corporation's profitability relative to the profitability of other companies in the same industry by revealing how much profit a company generates with the money shareholders have invested (investor equity). The higher a company's ROE, the more that company creates for its shareholders, and the better return they can expect on their investment. ROE is calculated as follows:

Return on Equity = Net Income/Shareholder's Equity

Let's evaluate two hypothetical, high-end jewelry stores located in our local mall (Store A and Store B). Both stores generated $5 million in profits (net income or earnings) last year. However, Store A generated its profits with $20 million in shareholder equity (from shares sold), while Store B needed $50 million in investor equity to obtain the same result. Using the ROE formula provided above, Store A boasted an ROE of 25% ($5/$20), while Store B's ROE was only 10% ($5/$50). Store A therefore, was more efficient and profitable than Store B because it created more profit for each of each of its shareholders.

A company's ROE is often compared to that of other companies in the same industry, whereas EPS (see below) and P/E ratios are better used as a barometer of whether the shares themselves are over or undervalued.

We will require our stocks to have ROEs of 15% or higher. This is generally considered a financially healthy statistic. Other ratio requirements are also set because they meet the generally accepted "healthy financially" standards of analysts.

Earnings Per Share (EPS)

EPS is the portion of a company's profit allocated to each outstanding share of common stock, and serves as a measure of a company's profitability:

$$EPS = [\text{Net Income} - \text{Dividends on Preferred Stock}] / \text{Average Outstanding Shares}$$

Let's look at two carpet companies. In 2012, Company A generated an annual profit of $1 million, while Company B generated twice that amount, or a $2 million annual profit in the same year. Company B, at least initially, looks like the better company/stock. Assume further that in 2012, both companies distributed $200,000 in dividends to its shareholders. However, Company A has 100,000 shares outstanding, while Company B has 300,000 shares outstanding. Let's do some quick math:

- EPS (Company A) = $1,000,000 − 200,000/100,000
= $8 per share
- EPS (Company B) = $2,000,000 - $200,000/300,000
= $6 per share
- For this ratio, Company A is the winner.

We will require our stocks to have positive EPS growth during the past 5 years and projected EPS growth of 10% or greater over the next 5 years. This demonstrates past EPS strength and analyst consensus for future EPS success.

Sales Growth

Sales growth represents the rate at which a company can, or has, achieved by increasing output and enhancing sales. A generally accepted yardstick for financially sound companies is a sales growth rate of 10% or better. **We will require our shares to have achieved a positive sales growth rate over the past 5 years.**

Price to Book (P/B Ratio)

This ratio compares the price of a stock to the value of the company assuming the company is broken up and sold today. This ratio is calculated by dividing the current closing price of the stock by the book value (total value of the company's assets that shareholders would receive if a company were liquidated) per share for the most recent quarter:

$$\text{P/B Ratio} = \text{Stock Price/ Total Assets} - \text{Intangible assets } and$$
$$Liabilities$$

Assume one of our local jewelry stores has a book value of $2 million, with 200,000 shares outstanding and a current share price of $30. We would calculate the P/B ratio as follows:

- Book value = $2,000,000/200,000 = $10 per share
- The P/B ratio = $30/$10 = 3

A generally accepted P/B for healthy companies is "3" or lower. **We therefore will require our securities to have P/B Ratios of "4" or less.**

40

Summary

Fundamental Requirements for Our Wealth-Building Portfolios

- PEG ratios of "2" or less

- ROEs of 15% or higher

- Positive EPS growth during the past 5 years

- Projected EPS growth of 10% or greater over the next 5 years

- Achieved a positive sales growth rate over the past 5 years

- P/B Ratios of "4" or less

Review

Descriptive Requirements for Our Wealth-Building Portfolio (from Chapter 1)

- Share price of $15 or higher

- Market-cap of $2 billion or greater

- Average daily trading volume of 500,000 shares per day or higher

Online Stock Screeners:

Screening for Stocks that Satisfy Our Portfolio Requirements

At this point, you might be asking yourself, "How do I know which stocks to analyze," "where do I even begin," or "what am I supposed to do with all of these wealth-building portfolio rules?" Not to worry –the wonderful world of online stock screeners has our backs! As the name implies, stock screeners are software tools, usually Internet based, that allow investors to search or "screen" for investments based on pre-determined criteria, often referred to as "filters." As such, stock screeners narrow the investment universe from thousands of stocks, mutual funds, ETFs, etc. to a select few that meet investors' needs. *Thus far*, our requirements for selecting stocks for our wealth-building portfolio include the descriptive requirements highlighted in Chapter 1 (e.g. share price of $15 or higher, etc.), and the fundamental requirements discussed in this chapter (e.g. PEG ratio of "2" or less, etc.). With the right stock screener, we can simply plug in the values of our requirements (a few more rules will be added in later chapters) and out pops a list of stocks screened to meet our defined criteria.

Almost all online brokers offer, at the least, a basic stock-screening tool (you will ultimately have to open an account with an online broker in order to buy and sell stocks, as discussed in Chapter 7 and Appendix II). In addition, there are many free online stock screeners that can be found around on the Internet. The sophistication and usefulness of these screeners vary depending on investor needs. For purposes of our wealth-building portfolio, I prefer to use the free online stock screener offered at www.finviz.com (FINVIZ), which allows us to screen stocks for the descriptive and fundamental requirements discussed thus far, as well as the *additional screens* that will be discussed in later chapters (such as our *technical requirements*, discussed in Chapter 3). Figure 1 is a screenshot depicting how to incorporate our descriptive and fundamental criteria into the FINVIZ.com stock screener. Note that to get to the screen depicted in Figure 1, click on the **"Screener"** tab (top left) and **"All"** tab (top/middle, under the "Signal" scroll down option). You should now see a screen similar to the one depicted in Figure 1[1], which includes fields for all nine of the portfolio rule requirements discussed thus far. The nine applicable fields corresponding to our requirements are also highlighted in Figure 1 for ease of reference. Populate the fields with the appropriate rule values, and the screen will automatically update as parameters are added.

Figure 1 – Filtering for Securities that Meet Our Descriptive and Fundamental Requirements Using FINVIZ

---

[1] Please note that the right side of Figure 1 cut off, however all necessary information is depicted therein.

Chapter 3

Technical Analysis –
The Power of the Charts

Chapter Outline- Section 1:
Technical Analysis for our Wealth-Building Portfolio

- Chapter introduction
- Simple moving averages (SMAs) – our key technical indicator
- Technical requirements of our wealth-building portfolio
- Stock charts and the application of our technical requirements
- Moving average crossovers
- Using FINVIZ to screen for stocks that meet our technical requirements
- Summary of our technical requirements for our wealth-building portfolios

Chapter Outline- Section 2:
Technical analysis for short-term investment strategies

- Stockcharts.com: a free site to construct price charts
- Types of price charts
- Moving averages
- Moving Average Convergence Divergence (MACD)
- MACD Histogram
- Stochastic Oscillator

- Volume
- Constructing a technical chart
- Technical Analysis and Short-Term Investing: Putting It All Together With Sample Charts

Wealth-Building Rules in this Chapter

- Uptrending 50-day and 200-day moving averages
- 50-day SMA above the 200-day SMA
- Stock price above the 50-day SMA

Section 1: Technical Analysis for Our Wealth-Building Portfolio

Chapter introduction

Despite all the colorful and exotic tools it employs, technical analysis really is quite simple – it's the study of historical stock prices in an attempt to predict future stock price movements. Technical traders believe there is no reason to analyze a company's fundamentals because this information is already accounted for in the stock's price, which can be found on charts and other tools that graphically depict past price patterns that may suggest future activity. Although generally regarded as the polar opposite of fundamental analysis, technical analysis is an equally essential tool in the armamentarium of stock investors, and will be not only helping to constructing our wealth-building portfolio, but also in our entry and exit strategy determinations. Accordingly, technical analysis represents the next screen in the stock selection process for our wealth-building portfolio.

This chapter will be presented in two sections. **The first section discusses technical analysis as it applies to constructing our wealth-building portfolio and long-term stock investment strategy, which is what this book is all about. This section is by far the briefer segment of the two, and is what you need to focus on the most.** The second section is devoted to a more sophisticated level of technical analysis; one that can be applied to *shorter-term* investment strategies that (depending on your level of experience investing in the stock market) may be more suitable as your experience with the intricacies of the market grows.

The Simple Moving Average (SMA) – Our Key Technical Indicator

Overview

After identifying the specific descriptive and fundamental requirements for our wealth-building portfolios (outlined in the two preceding chapters), we then must utilize technical analysis to ensure these stocks are in favorable price trends (prices making higher highs and higher lows). As they say on Wall Street, "the trend is your friend," and one of the best ways to identify a stock's trend is to analyze the *moving averages* of its price. Moving averages are technical indicators that chart the average value of a security's price (usually the closing price) over a set time period. In other words, a moving average shows the average of stock's up-and-down price movements during a specific period of time. All the moving average really does is smooth out the direction of a stock's price trend so that the wild day-to-day price and volume fluctuations don't throw off your market perspective. *They identify trends* but are not necessarily predictive of future price movement.

There are two main types of moving averages used in technical analysis: the Simple Moving Average (SMA) and the Exponential Moving Average (EMA). The EMA, in addition to other technical indicators for shorter-term strategies, is discussed later on in this chapter. **For our wealth-building portfolios, the SMA is the only technical indicator we need to familiarize ourselves with.** So let's take a closer look at the SMA, and then discuss how we will use this indicator to screen for stocks best suited for our wealth-building portfolios.

The SMA is the average price of a security over a specific number of periods, which (unlike the EMA) gives equal weighting to each price in the data set. For example, a 50-day SMA is simply today's closing price added to the prior 49 days' closing prices. Divide that number by 50 and the answer is what's plotted on today's chart (note that today's closing price, even though it's the most recent price, is not weighted any greater than the closing price for day 49). Old closing prices are dropped as new closing prices become available; thus, the average "moves" over time (don't worry, computers do all the calculations and charting for us).

Basic SMA Example

Let's create a simple example as to how moving averages are calculated. In this hypothetical, Stock A has had the following closing prices the past 5 days:

- $7.00 (5 days ago)
- $7.50 (4 days ago)
- $8.00 (3 days ago)
- $7.50 (2 days ago)
- $8.50 (today)

48

We add up the 5 closing prices to get $38.50, and then divide by 5 to calculate a 5-day (5-d) SMA of $7.70. That SMA price point ($7.70) gets plotted on the chart. Notice that today's share price of $8.50 is *above* the SMA price of $7.70, *which is a bullish signal.* This last point is an important point one that bears repeating: *a bullish (buy) signal exists when the current price of a security is above the current price of its SMA.* This notion is the linchpin of one of the technical rules for our wealth-building portfolio, which will be discussed shortly.

> Note: If we were to calculate the 5-day SMA for Stock A *the following day* (assume stock A closed at $9.00 the following day), the 5 closing prices we now have to add are: $9.00 + $8.50 + $7.50 + $8.00 + $7.50 = $40.50. We then divide $40.50 by 5, which gives us a new SMA of $8.10. Notice how $7.00 was *not* included in our calculation when we recalculated the SMA the *following day*. That's because SMAs drop old prices as new prices become available; thus the average "moves" over time, as stated earlier in this chapter. If we were to continue to calculate Stock A's 5-day SMA over time, and plotted that SMA on a chart, we would generate a SMA that is smoother (have *less* dramatic spikes and drops) than the *actual* prices of Stock A plotted over the same time period. Remember, moving averages smooth out the direction of a stock's price trend so that the wild day-to-day price fluctuations don't throw off your market perspective.

Now, let's use the same prices from our initial hypothetical example and calculate a shorter-term SMA for Stock A – its 3-day SMA. The last 3 trading day prices add up to $24.00 ($8.50 + $7.50 + $8.00). We then divide by 3 to get a 3-day SMA of $8.00. Note that the shorter-term SMA (3-day) is above the longer-term SMA (5-day), *also a bullish signal*. This point is also echoed in the technical rules for our wealth-building portfolio (discussed shortly); that is, *we have a bullish signal when the shorter-term SMA is above the longer-term SMA.*

Long-Term vs. Short-Term SMAs

As alluded to in the prior hypothetical example, SMAs, as with all moving averages, can be short-term or long-term depending on the type of trading strategy being employed. Short-term moving averages help gauge the short-term direction of a stock, while longer-term moving averages take a bigger picture view. Generally speaking, long-term trends use moving averages greater than 50 days, such as the 100-day or 150-day moving averages. However, the 200-day moving average (200-d) may be the granddaddy of them all, as it is widely viewed as a measure of long-term market sentiment; stocks trading above the 200-d are generally considered healthy, while those trading below it are viewed as anemic. The 50-day moving average (50-d) is widely used to help define intermediate term trends. Together, *the 50-d and 200-d are most widely used moving average indicators* in spotting stock trends as they relate to longer-term investment strategies such as our wealth-building plan.

For purposes of our wealth-building portfolio, we are long-term investors and therefore are more concerned with where our stocks will be priced later on down the road. As long-term investors, the 200-d is an ideal *long-term* SMA to use in connection with our wealth building strategy. Likewise, the 50-d SMA, although generally considered an intermediate technical indicator, serves as the ideal *short-term* indicator for conservative, long-term investment goals. For these reasons, the 50-d and 200-d are the two SMAs we will use to assist us in selecting stocks for our wealth-building portfolio.

Technical Requirements for Our Wealth-Building Portfolios

One of the things I like most about our wealth-building strategy is that it is simple yet very effective if implemented properly. To that end, the 50-d and 200-d SMAs are the *only* technical indicators we need to concern ourselves with when selecting securities for our wealth-building portfolios. Even better, there are *only three* rules associated with these SMAs that we need to apply when selecting our securities:

- We will only select securities that have uptrending 50-d and 200-d SMAs (higher highs and higher lows)
- We will only select securities whose current price is above its 50-d SMA
- We will only select securities whose 50-d SMA is currently above the 200-d SMA

Let's Pause to Make Sure We're On the Same Page . . .

I began this chapter emphasizing that technical analysis involves the use of stock charts to analyze the past prices of a security in an effort to predict its future prices or at least identify trends. Thus, in a minute we will learn to analyze a basic stock chart using the technical indicators (50-d and 200-d SMAs) and portfolio security selection rules discussed thus far. However, before we do, let's pause for a moment and go over a few brief points to ensure that we are all on the same page:

- First, as with the rules discussed in the preceding chapters (e.g. descriptive and fundamental rules), and additional rules that will be discussed in chapters to come, we will use the three technical requirements discussed in the preceding section in conjunction with a stock-screening tool (e.g. FINVIZ) to generate a list of securities that meet our specified criteria (and thus are potential candidates for our wealth-building portfolio). Given the use of a stock-screening tool, our wealth-building plan does *not*, at least literally, require us to create or analyze stock charts. However, if your goal is to become a serious and successful investor, I *strongly believe* that, at the least, you should learn to understand and interpret our three technical wealth-building requirements as they appear on stock charts. As you gain experience investing in the stock market, you may want to implement additional investment strategies (or even supplement the wealth- building strategy outlined in this book) with alternative investment strategies, many of which may very well be technical in nature. If you do not learn how to read and interpret basic technical indicators (e.g. SMAs) on stock charts, you will be doing yourself a great disservice in this regard.

- Second, for purposes of analyzing stock charts in conjunction with our portfolio rules, we need only concern ourselves with *three* data sets: (i) the 50-d SMA; (ii) the 200-d SMA; and (iii) historical prices of the stock we are analyzing. That's it. While our primary focus should be on reading and understanding stock chart basics, should you ever endeavor to create your own stock chart, bear in mind that all three of these data sets will be automatically generated for you after you specify the portfolio rules in your charting software. You do not have to do any math to create the any of these data sets, and you will have the applicable charting software to do so at your fingerprints, whether it be software offered by the brokerage firm you use (e.g. E*TRADE, Charles Schwab, etc. . . more on brokerage firms later on in this book), or by reputable online websites such as stockcharts.com that offer free charting services.

- Lastly, bear in mind that the technical rules discussed in this chapter, the fundamental and descriptive rules discussed in the preceding chapters, and additional rules which will discussed in the chapters to come, will all be implemented in a stock screener (e.g. FINVIZ) *simultaneously*, although these rules are discussed piecemeal on a per chapter basis in this book. This will generate a list of stocks that meet *all* the rules and requirements we specify.

Stock Charts and the Application of Our Technical Requirements

We are now ready to analyze a stock chart and apply the technical rules discussed in this chapter thus far. Figure 2 (created using the free charting tools offered by stockcharts.com) depicts a one-year *line chart* (types of charts discussed below) of AOS Smith Corp. (AOS), a NYSE-listed stock. Figure 2 also contains AOS' 50-d SMA and 200-d SMA over the same time period. By "one-year price chart" I mean that the historical daily closing prices of AOS have been plotted from the present day (i.e. the most recent closing price of AOS as of the date the chart was created, or in this example November 16, 2012) dating back one year (to November 16, 2011). Note how the 50-d SMA (blue line) and 200-d SMA (red line) lines are smoother than the actual prices of AOS *(top line on chart). Also note how the 50-d SMA reacts more quickly to spikes and drops in the price of AOS. This is because the shorter the moving average time frame, the less the lag it will have in relation to the current stock's movement. Last point before we discuss our technical rules; this chart is what is called a "line" chart. I created this chart in line chart format for illustrative purposes; however, as will be discussed in the next section of this chapter, stock prices can be charted in a variety of formats, and do not necessarily have to be in this particular format (and in fact, usually are not).

Figure 2 – AOS Met the Technical Requirements for Our Wealth-Building Portfolio in Nov. 2012

Now let's analyze this chart in the context of our portfolio rules. Looking at Figure 2, does AOS pass all of our technical rule requirements? Let's take a closer look:

Step 1: Does AOS must have uptrending 50-d and 200-d SMAs? In other words, do both SMAs exhibit a trend of having higher highs and higher lows? As we can see from Figure 2, both the 50-d and 200-d are clearly trending upwards, so AOS does in fact meet our first technical requirement.

Step 2: Is AOS's *current* stock price above its 50-d SMA? AOS' "current" stock price is its most recent closing price. In this example, AOS closed at $59.57 when I created Figure 2 on November 16, 2012, and the price of its corresponding 50-d SMA was $57.87 on this date (see black/blue prices at top left corner of Figure 2, and black/blue encircled prices on right side). Because AOS' stock prices are higher than its 50-d SMA, AOS passes our second technical requirement. One more rule to pass!

Step 3: Is AOS' 50-d SMA currently above its 200-d SMA? Again, a quick look at our charts easily gives us the answer. AOS' 50-d SMA of $57.87 is well above $49.75, its current 200-d SMA (see prices in black/red at top left corner of Figure 2, and black/red encircled prices on right side). Thus, AOS passes our third and final technical rule requirement, and thus, from a technical standpoint, is a candidate for our wealth-building portfolio (it still must pass all of our other rules, however).

A Word on Moving Average Crossovers

There are two additional signals, called *moving average crossovers*, which we should be aware of. A moving average crossover occurs when a short-term SMA (e.g. 50-day) crosses either above or below a long-term SMA (e.g. 200-day). In short, the rules of thumb for moving average crossovers are as follows:

- If the 50-d SMA crosses above the 200-d SMA, we have a bullish, or buy signal, because this scenario signals upward momentum in the stock's price. Note the bullish moving average crossover in January of 2012 in Figure 2.

- If the 50-d SMA crosses below the 200-d SMA, we have a bearish, or sell signal, because this scenario is indicative of downward momentum in the stock's price.

Bullish crossovers are *not* essential for a security to be eligible for our wealth-building portfolio, however it is important to recognize what they are and when they occur so that appropriate action can be taken. Personally, I would never enter a position for a stock that has recently had a bearish moving average crossover. On the other hand, if a bearish crossover occurred for a security I *already owned*, I might consider taking a look at possibly utilizing an exit strategy to sell my position in the stock (more on exit strategies later on in this book). Similarly, a bullish moving average crossover, while not a requirement for our portfolio, may lead me to give that particular security serious consideration, assuming it meets all of our other portfolio strategy requirements.

Using FINVIZ to Apply the Technical Requirements for Our Portfolio

Now that we learned how to use charts to screen for stocks that meet our technical rule requirements, let's move on to the easy part – inputting our technical rules into a stock screener (in this case, FINVIZ, which is what I use). Figure 3, a screenshot from FINVIZ.com, depicts in yellow the fields germane to *all* the wealth-building portfolio rule requirements we have learned thus far (descriptive, fundamental and technical), with a screen requirement for the 200-d SMA to be below the 50-d SMA, which will ensure all stocks that pass this screen have positive momentum. Likewise, we will also screen for stocks with prices above the 50-d SMA. A stock trading above its 50-d SMA which in turn is trading above the 200-d SMA will generally be an uptrending stock. Pretty simple, huh?

Figure 3 - Filtering for Our Technical Requirements Using FINVIZ

Summary of our technical requirements for our wealth-building portfolio

- Uptrending 50-d and 200-d SMAs (higher highs and higher lows)
- Current Stock price above the 50-d SMA
- We will only select securities whose 50-d SMA is currently above the 200-d SMA

57

The material discussed thus far in this chapter *is all you need to know for our long-term, wealth-building strategy.* At this point, feel free to turn directly to Chapter 4. However, if you would like to learn about other technical indicators, read on. Please note that although the remaining information in this chapter is not applicable to our wealth-building portfolio, you may find it extremely useful for employing *shorter-term* investment strategies.

Section 2: Technical Analysis for Short-Term Investment Strategies

Stockcharts.com: a free site to construct price charts

In the future, should you decide to incorporate a more sophisticated level of technical analysis into your stock strategies you will need to develop the skill to create a price chart based on the parameters you decide to utilize.

A great *free* site to use for creating technical charts is:

www.stockcharts.com

This site was used to generate the chart depicted in Figure 2. The lower portion of the screenshot in Figure 2 shows you how to set up such a chart. All other criteria below "moving averages" (not in this screenshot) were placed as "none" or "off"

There are a myriad of technical indicators that can be used for short-term investment strategies. If and when you choose to engage in shorter-term investment strategies, the ones you choose may differ from those that I prefer to incorporate into my short-term strategies. In this portion of Chapter 3, I will discuss the four short-term technical parameters that I use to select stocks for my covered call writing strategy (a short term strategy discussed later in this book, and in my first three books), and how I use these parameters to make my investment decisions. These parameters can be applied to other shorter-term strategies as well.

However, before we get into a detailed explanation of these short-term parameters, it's important that we first review the different types of *charts* that we can use when conducting technical analysis.

Line Charts, Bar Charts and Candlestick Charts

As you now know, technical analysis is the study of past price movements in an attempt to predict future price movements or trends. Historical price patterns are graphically depicted on *price charts*, which are then studied in conjunction with other technical indicators to make these predictions. In the short-term, investor emotions tend have a greater impact on stock prices and trends, irrespective of whether these emotions are rational. Thus, stock prices tend to be more erratic in the short-term. For this reason, when employing technical analysis, particularly for a short-term investment strategy, it is important that you are comfortable with the common chart types used to study these price movements.

Line Charts

The *Line chart* (as seen in Figure 2) is a very basic chart created by connecting a series of closing prices of a particular security with a line. Line charts do not provide visual information of the trading range for the individual points such as the high, low and opening prices of the day (or other time frame). Figure 4 depicts what a standard Line chart looks like:

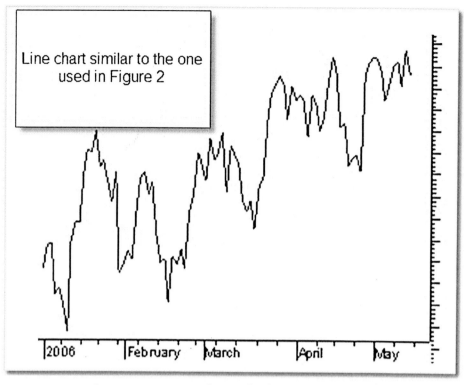

Figure 4 - Line Chart of Closing Prices

Candlestick Charts

Candlestick charts emphasize the relationship between the daily opening and closing prices of a stock each day over a particular time period of time. As the name implies, Candlestick charts are comprised of individual candlestick lines. Each candlestick displays the high, low, opening and close prices of a particular security for a specific time period, which can be as long as a month or as short as one minute, depending on the purpose for which the chart is to be used (*daily* Candlestick charts, which represent a full trading session, are the most popular). One of the first things you will notice when you view a Candlestick chart is that the candlesticks are one of two *colors*, depending on whether or not the stock closed at a price higher than it opened that day. Although the color schemes of

60

a Candlestick chart may vary depending on the chart provider, generally speaking:

- If a candlestick is white (or green) the stock closed higher than it opened; and
- If a candlestick is black (or red) the stock closed lower than it opened.

Figure 5 highlights the components of two individual candlesticks – one depicting that the stock closed at a higher price than it opened (white), and the other depicting that the stock closed lower than it opened (black):

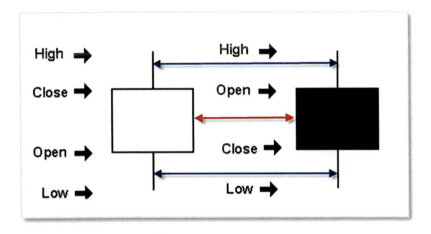

Figure 5 - Two Individual Candlesticks

Let's take a closer look at the information that can be derived from the two candlestick lines in Figure 5:

- The middle or "fat" portion (red arrows) is called the *body* (or "*real body*") and represents the range between the opening and closing prices of the stock. If the body is white (or green), the stock closed higher than its open. Here, the opening price is the lowest point on the body, and the closing price is the highest point on the real

body. If the body is black (or red), the stock closed lower than its open. Here, the opening price is the highest point of the real body, and the closing price is the lowest point of the real body
- The thin lines extending out from the bottom and tops of the body are called *shadows* (upper and lower) and represent the session's high and low prices (blue double-sided arrows)
- In sum, a white (or green) candlestick is a positive or bullish sign, and a black (or red) candlestick is a negative or bearish sign

Note: A *weekly* candlestick is based on Monday's open, the weekly high-low range and Friday's close.

Figure 6 depicts what a typical daily Candlestick chart looks like:

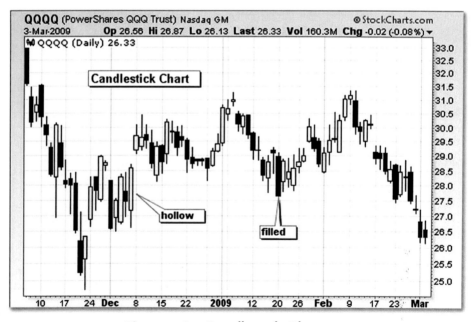

Figure 6 - Candlestick Chart

Note that the black (filled) candlesticks indicate a stock price that closed lower than its open and a white (hollow) candlestick is indicative of a daily price that closed higher than its open.

Bar Chart

Like the Candlestick chart, the Bar chart consists of session high and lows, in addition to the opening and closing prices. Each bar on a Bar chart represents price performance for a specific period, which (like candlesticks) can vary depending on the purpose for which the chart is to be used, though *daily* Bar charts (i.e. a full trading session) are the most popular. The Bar chart is also referred to as the "Open-High-Low- Close" chart, or the "OHLC" chart for short.

Figure 7 highlights the characteristics of an individual bar found on a typical Bar chart:

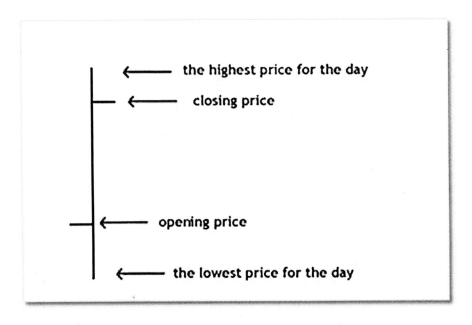

Figure 7 – Single Bar (or OHLC Bar)

As you can see, the information provided by bar is similar to the information provided by candlesticks. To establish the relationship between the opening and closing prices on the Bar chart, we look at the *horizontal lines* to the right and left of the vertical line. In Candlestick charts, we look for the color differences between the bodies of the candlesticks. Many charting applications will also color code the bars on a Bar chart as either red or black:

- Red: Depicts a lower close than the *previous day's close*
- Black: Depicts a higher close than the *previous day's close*

Bar Chart vs. Candlestick Chart

The Bar and Candlestick charts share several important characteristics. The most notable of these similarities are as follows:

- Both display the high, low, open and close prices for the specified time frame
- Neither chart reflects the sequence of events between the open and close
- Both charts provide much more information than the line chart

The Bar and Candlestick charts also contain the following notable differences:

- In Candlestick charts, the relationship between the opening and closing prices is depicted by the color of the body, whereas Bar charts depict that relationship with small horizontal ticks projecting from the left and right sides of its vertical line of price points

- The Bar chart places greater emphasis on the closing price of the stock in relation to the *prior* period's (day, week etc.) closing price. In contrast, the Candlestick chart emphasizes the closing price as it relates to the opening price on the *same* day (or week, depending on the time frame used). I prefer the former and this is the primary reason I prefer the Bar chart, however the difference is negligible. A colored bar will provide both daily and previous time frame contrasts.

Since so many investors use the *www.stockcharts.com* site, let's view both (figures 8 and 9) chart patterns as created from this site:

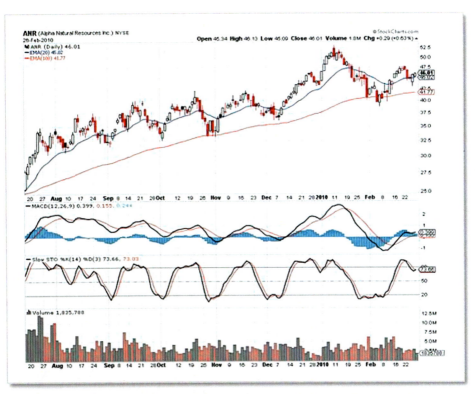

Figure 8 - Candlestick Chart for Alpha Natural Resources, Inc. (ANR)

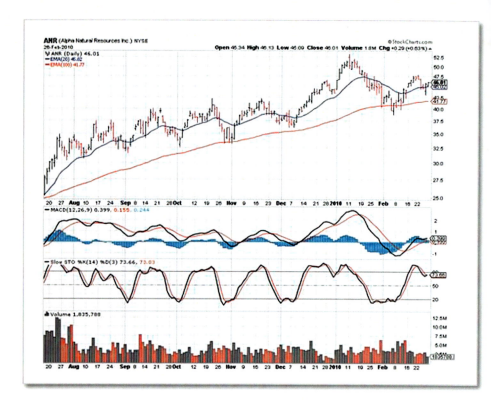

Figure 9 - Bar Chart for ANR

Figures 8 and 9 depict the price history of Alpha Natural resources, Inc. for the same time frames. Both are daily charts which I feel are best for short-term investment strategies. These charts also demonstrate the technical parameters I will discuss in this section including the moving averages (blue and red lines at the top of the chart), the MACD in the middle of the chart, the Stochastic Oscillator and Volume towards the bottom of the charts. These parameters will be detailed shortly.

Conclusion

In short, both the Candlestick and Bar charts offer much more information than the line charts. Some chartists prefer the color feature of the candlestick bodies, while others prefer the emphasis on closing price comparison with the previous period offered by the bar charts. You can't go wrong with either one. My advice is to select the chart you like and use it consistently, so that ultimately, reading a technical chart will take only a few seconds.

Next we will discuss the four technical parameters that I prefer to use for my shorter-term investing strategies, which include: (1) moving averages; (2) the Moving Average Convergence Divergence (MACD); (3) the Stochastic Oscillator and; (4) volume. Using multiple parameters provides trend-identifying as well as momentum identifying information along with volume confirmation. A detailed discussion of each parameter follows.

1.   Moving Averages

For me, of the four technical parameters that I use for shorter-term investing, the moving average is king, with the others playing confirming roles. Each indicator by itself will not suffice, but as a whole, they paint a very important picture relating to our buy-sell decisions. First, let's briefly review some key terminology to ensure we are all speaking the same language.

Definitions (some terms are review from section 1)

- *Downtrend* - the price movement of a stock is in a downward direction, forming a series of lower highs and lower lows
- *Exponential Moving Average (EMA)* - similar to an SMA except more weight is given to the most recent prices
- *Moving Average (MA)* – the average value of a security's price over a set period of time, used to

measure momentum and define areas of possible support and resistance

- *Resistance* - the price level which a stock has had difficulty rising above, and at which a large amount of sell-side interest exists (sellers tend to outnumber buyers)
- *Sideways Pattern (consolidation)* - horizontal price movement in an equity (the forces of supply and demand are equal), which indicates a stock's inability to establish either an uptrend or a downtrend. Note: *The moving average parameter is less reliable in a sideways pattern.*
- *Simple Moving Average (SMA)* - a moving average that gives equal weight to each day's (or other time frame used like week or month) price data
- *Support* - the price level at which a stock has difficulty falling below, and at which a large amount of buy-side interest exists (buyers tend to outnumber sellers)
- *Uptrend* - the price movement of a stock is in an upward direction, forming a series of higher highs and higher lows

Simple Moving Average vs. Exponential Moving Average

With shorter-term strategies, I prefer the EMA to the SMA because the EMA reacts more quickly to changes in the stock price. Additionally, using the EMA also helps to avoid "false positives" in which a stock jumps above the slower moving SMA but not above the quicker moving EMA. To many technicians, when a price moves above its moving average, a bullish signal is confirmed. Figure 10 (from www.stockcharts.com) illustrates this point. Figure 10 depicts a daily Bar chart depicting Apple Inc.'s (AAPL) stock price, 100-d SMA (blue) and 100-d EMA (red) for the period of November 2008 through February 2009. As shown in Figure 10, AAPL's stock price broke through and above its 100-d SMA during the first two weeks of February 2009. As *long-term* investors, we would normally view this scenario as a bullish (buy) signal. Thus, assuming (as *long-term* investors) we bought AAPL using the SMA as our technical indicator, we would not be concerned when, approximately three weeks later, AAPL's stock price dropped back below its SMA, and in fact will see our long-term strategy pay off when the stock soars in mid-March.

The scenario is quite different if a short-term investor was looking to buy *and* sell AAPL in February 2009 for a quick profit. For *short-term* investors who relied on the SMA in this example, what initially appeared to be a buy signal (AAPL's stock price initially crossing above its SMA) in the first half of February 2009 turned out to be a "false positive" because the stock subsequently dropped back below its SMA two weeks later. Thus, the short-term investor who bought AAPL when its price crossed its SMA (and who, in this example, does not want own AAPL heading into the month of March) ultimately sold his AAPL stock at a loss before the price increased again in March. As Figure 10 demonstrates, this "false positive" *would have been avoided* had the *100-d EMA* (red) been used by the short-term investor. This is because in early February 2009, unlike the SMA, AAPL's stock price *never crossed the EMA*, which started adjusting upwards faster than the SMA as the AAPL's stock price appreciated. This would be an important distinction to consider for those of you who decide to use shorter-term strategies, one of which will be discussed towards the end of this book.

Figure 10 - Simple vs. Exponential Moving Averages

The parameters I prefer to use (for short-term strategies) are the 20-d and 100-d EMAs. I will be discussing a short-term conservative stock and option strategy later in the book called *covered call writing* but these moving average parameters apply to other short-term strategies as well. The 20-d approximates the number of trading days in the 1-month stock option contract. The 100-d represents 20 weeks (5 trading days/week), or five months, and gives us a longer-term perspective to compare with the shorter term 20-d EMA. I like to use both for strategies of one month duration. When viewing the moving average indicator, *we like to see the 20-d above the 100-d EMA and the price bars at or above the 20-d EMA.* This shows a positive upward momentum and favors (but does not guarantee) continued price appreciation. This is similar to our long-term technical requirement where we want uptrending moving averages and the shorter term (50-d SMA) above the longer term (200-d SMA) and the price bars above the shorter term SMA. Moving averages are considered *lagging indicators*, which means they trail the price action of a stock. Thus, *moving averages confirm trends but do not predict them.*

However, once a trend is identified, we want to be part of that wild ride to cash profits! Figure 11 depicts the same chart of AAPL illustrated in Figure 10, except here the 20-d EMA and 100-d EMA are used:

Figure 11 - Short Term (blue) vs. Long Term (red) EMAs

Notice in Figure 11 that at the end of March, when the short term 20-d EMA (blue) moved above longer term 100-d EMA (red), the stock went to the moon with the price bars at or above the 20-d EMA. The red arrow shows the point of the crossover and the blue arrow shows the price appreciation after that bullish signal.

When to Use Moving Averages - Practical Application

Moving averages have little value when the stock price is in a period of consolidation (moving sideways without establishing a definitive trend). In these instances, we turn to our confirming indicators (about to be discussed) to either include or exclude the stock from consideration. When the stock is downtrending (November through January in Figure 11), we exclude the stock and opt for another equity. If the stock is trending upwards, the price bars are at or above the 20-d EMA and the short term EMA is above the longer term EMA, we have a strong buy signal. This buy signal is even stronger if confirmed by MACD, stochastics and volume (discussed shortly). Most winning stocks never make a serious breach below the 20-d EMA which is now considered "support" (discussed shortly) for the share price. This staying power above the 20-d EMA is indicative of institutional support for that equity On the other hand, when a stock drops sharply below support (the 20-d EMA) on high volume, these major players (mutual funds, banks, insurance companies, pension funds etc.) are starting to move out of this stock and so should we.

When identifying stocks for our short-term watch lists and portfolios, we look for uptrending price patterns and utilize moving averages to confirm these trends. In an ideal situation, the price bars (OHLC) bounce off and above the short-term (20-day) exponential moving average. When this occurs, the moving average is serving as *support* for the price of the stock. In the inverse situation, where the price is trading below the moving average and bouncing off and under this average, the 20-d EMA is serving as *resistance* for the equity price. Support and resistance are discussed next in more detail:

Support

Price levels or ranges at which there is sufficient demand for a stock to cause a halt in a downward trend and turn the trend up. Support levels indicate the price (or price ranges) at which most investors feel that price of a security will move higher. Think of support levels as floors or areas where a declining stock is likely to bounce off and move higher (at least temporarily). Figure 12 depicts a daily Candlestick chart of Amazon com., Inc. (AMZN) in which there is support slightly below $60. Note in Figure 12 how AMZN's price continuously turns back upwards once it dips just below $60:

Figure 12 - Trendline Serving as Support

As previously stated, support can be represented by moving averages (depicted in Figures 15 and 16, to be discussed shortly), or in the form of a *trendline* (a line connecting a series of descending tops, descending bottoms, ascending tops, or ascending bottoms) as shown in figure 12.

Resistance

Price levels or ranges at which there is a large enough supply of stock available to cause a halt in the upward price trend and turn the trend down. Resistance levels indicate the prices (or price ranges) at which most investors feel the price of a security will move lower. Think of resistance levels as ceilings or areas where a rallying stock is likely to run into trouble and be turned back (at least temporarily). Figure 13 depicts a daily Bar chart Eli Lilly & Co. (LLY) in which there is resistance slightly above $75. Note how the price of LLY tends to trend upwards until it hits its resistance level, at which point it is turned back down:

Figure 13 - Trendline Serving as Resistance

When seeking to locate the greatest performing stocks in the greatest performing industries we search for price patterns in an uptrend. *An uptrend is established when a security forms a series of higher highs and higher lows.* The Bar chart in Figure 14 illustrates an uptrend in EMC Corp. (EMC) from July 1996 through February, 2000.

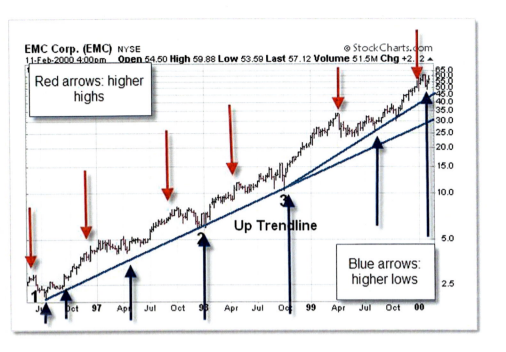

Figure 14 - Uptrending Price Pattern using a trendline

When uptrends, such as the one depicted in Figure 14, are identified in normal market conditions, our chances for price appreciation increase. Remember, "The trend is your friend"!

Figure 15 is a daily Line chart of STEC, Inc. (STEC), which illustrates an uptrending <u>moving average serving as support</u> for the price of this equity:

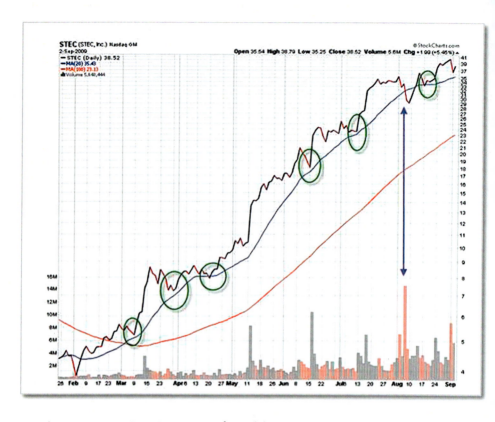

Figure 15 - STEC- Uptrending Moving Average Serving as Support

I constructed this chart as a line chart to show another perspective demonstrating the price bouncing off the uptrending 20-d EMA. The green circles depict areas of support. Note that in early August (purple double-side arrow) the chart shows that the price of this stock had a large drop on high volume (tall red bar at the bottom of the chart). The price temporarily dropped below the 20-d EMA. This was the result of a disappointing earnings report and exemplifies the impact these reports can have on share price. STEC reported earnings on August 4th and the market reacted negatively. We will discuss these reports and many other factors that can impact share price later in this book. In this case, we have a series of bullish signals as share price continued to bounce off an uptrending moving average. This trend was interrupted by a specific event (earnings report) that we must factor in our short-term strategies but not necessarily into our longer term strategies.

Moving averages can also serve as *both* support and resistance. Figure 16, a 6-month chart of Netflix (NFLX), demonstrates how the moving averages (in this case, the 20-d 100-d EMAs) can represent both support and resistance:

Figure 16 - Moving Averages Serving as Support and Resistance

The four key stages demonstrated in Figure 16 are summarized below. Each numbered paragraph corresponds to the boxed numbers referenced in Figure 16:

1. In late July 2011, the price of NFLX breaks below support (the 20-d EMA/blue line) and continues to decline until it hits its 100-d EMA (red line) and bounces back upwards. The price continues to fluctuate between the 20-d EMA and the 100-d EMA through the earlier

part of the first week of August. Thus, during that time, the 20-d EMA served as resistance, while the 100-d EMA served as support.

2.   Towards the end of the first week of August 2011, the price of NFLX breaks above resistance (20-d EMA), and continues to trade in an uptrend through September to the beginning of October (highlighted by blue arrow). Note that during that time period, the 20-d EMA served as support.

3.   For the majority of October and November 2011 (yellow-highlighted area), NFLX demonstrates a sideways trading pattern with no definite up or downtrend. This is often referred to as *consolidation*.

4.   In mid-December 2011, the price of NFLX breaks below support (20-d EMA) and a downtrend begins as the 20-d EMA now serves as resistance.

Here are some key pointers by which we can use moving averages, and the concepts of support and resistance, to put *cash* in our pockets:

- Avoid equities in a downtrend [area 4 in Fig. 16]
- Avoid, or hold a conservative position in, a stock that is trending sideways [area 3 in Fig. 16]
- If a stock breaks through support (moves down) on high volume, be prepared to execute an exit strategy. Volume will be discussed later in the chapter
- If a stock breaks through resistance (moves up) on high volume, consider this a major technical positive

Summary – Moving Averages

One aspect of technical analysis is trend identification, which assists in making our buy-sell decisions. The primary tool we use in confirming trends is the moving average, which can also represent either support or resistance. Support and resistance are important technical indicators, because if breached, a bullish or bearish signal is confirmed. While the moving average is undoubtedly a useful technical tool, it is important to also keep in mind that it is a lagging indicator, and is not as predictive of future prices as some other technical indicators (such as the MACD, which is discussed shortly). But that's ok - we want as many friends as possible when investing our hard-earned money. As with all technical tools, **moving averages should not be used alone, but rather, in conjunction with our other technical indicators** to be discussed next.

2. *Moving Average Convergence Divergence (MACD)*

Technical analysis is as much an art as it is a science. No one parameter, by itself, will allow us to make our buy/sell decisions. But when you take all the indicators together, they paint a picture that is critical to maximizing our investment success. One of the simplest and most reliable of these parameters is the *Moving Average Convergence Divergence (MACD)*.

The MACD, the second of the four technical parameters I prefer for shorter-term investing, is a trend-following indicator that is also converted into a momentum indicator by subtracting a longer-term moving average from a shorter term moving average. The resulting plot forms a line that oscillates above and below zero without any upper or lower limits. So let's call it a *trend-following momentum indicator*. To simplify, the MACD gives us prior notice before the two EMAs cross. This notice can be used to discern bullish and bearish signals, as described below

MACD Formula (Frequently used Time Frames)

The stock's 26-d EMA is subtracted from its 12-d EMA. <u>Notice how much shorter-term our parameters are compared to our 50-day and 200-day moving averages we use for our wealth-building plan</u>. The resulting line created by these price points is called the MACD. A 9-d EMA of the MACD itself is also plotted and acts as a *trigger line* for buy and sell signals. The subtraction of the trigger line from the MACD itself is the basis for the *MACD Histogram*, an even quicker indicator than the MACD and the parameter I prefer to focus on. Let's look at Figure 17, which depicts these parameters:

Figure 17- MACD (Basic Chart)

The black arrow points to the MACD itself (black line), the red arrow points to the trigger line (red line), and the blue arrow points to the MACD Histogram (light blue bars). Note how the MACD oscillates above and below the zero line, which is also known as the *centerline.*

Bullish MACD Signals

There are three primary Bullish MACD signals we can look for to spot a good buying opportunity. These signals include: (1) Positive Divergence; (2) Bullish Moving Average Crossover; and (3) Bullish Centerline Crossover. This section will briefly discuss each of these signals in turn.

(1) *Positive Divergence* - the MACD begins to advance while the security itself remains in a downtrend, as depicted in Figure 18:

Figure 18 - MACD Positive Divergence

Note, in Figure 18, how the green MACD trend lines are positive (below the green arrow), while the red price trend lines remain negative. The green arrow also shows a positive MACD histogram (above zero).

(2) *Bullish Moving Average Crossover* – this occurs when the actual MACD moves above its 9-d EMA (the trigger line), as illustrated in Figure 19:

Figure 19 - Bullish Moving Average Crossover

Note in Figure 19 how the red arrows indicate when the MACD (black line) crosses above the trigger line (red line) while the histogram (light blue bars) turns positive. The price of the stock then heads to the moon (long red arrow).

(3) *Bullish Centerline Crossover* - the MACD moves above the zero line and into positive territory. This scenario can be used

as a confirmation of the positive divergence and bullish moving average crossover, as illustrated in Figure 20:

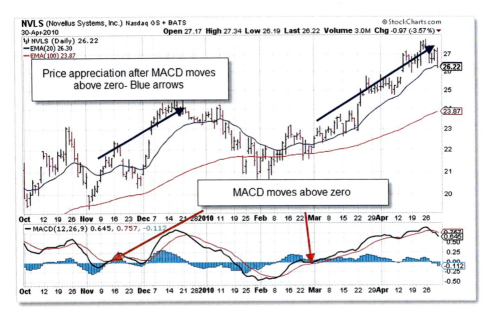

Figure 20 - Bullish Centerline Crossover

As shown in Figure 20, as the MACD moves above the zero line, the stock heads north, confirming a bullish centerline crossover.

Using a combination of these three bullish MACD signals can produce a more meaningful signal than using just one. I favor the MACD Histogram (detailed below), as it is an earlier indicator of a price change and can be easily spotted on a chart.

Bearish MACD Signals

Bearing MACD signals are effectively the reverse of the bullish signals discussed and, if confirmed by the other technical parameters, would represent a sell signal.

- Negative Divergence - MACD declines as security moves sideways or up.
- Bearish Moving Average Crossover - MACD declines below its 9-d EMA.
- Bearish Centerline Crossover - MACD moves below zero into negative territory.

Utilizing a combination of bearish signals will provide a more reliable indicator of a negative price change in the equity.

Advantages of MACD

- A reliable indicator that should be used in conjunction with other indicators
- Incorporates both trend and momentum into one indicator
- Uses exponential moving averages which eliminates some of the lag found in simple moving averages when using short-term strategies
- Foreshadows moves in the underlying security.

MACD Histogram (I prefer the MACD histogram to the MACD itself)

As noted above, the MACD Histogram represents the difference between the MACD and its trigger line, the 9-d EMA. It is plotted in the form of a histogram (bar graph) rendering divergences and centerline crossover easily identified. The histogram is an earlier indictor of potential price change and therefore the MACD parameter I prefer to focus on.

Bullish MACD Histogram signals include the following:

- A centerline crossover (i.e. the Histogram bars move above the centerline) into positive territory, which is equivalent to the MACD bullish moving average crossover (MACD moves above its trigger line)
- Increases in the positive Histogram show strengthening momentum
- Positive divergence of the Histogram will usually precede a positive move of the MACD itself

Bearish Histogram signals include the following:

- Negative Divergence- MACD declines as security moves sideways or up.
- Bearish Moving Average Crossover- MACD declines below its 9-d EMA.
- Bearish Centerline Crossover- MACD moves below zero into negative territory.

Utilizing a combination of bearish signals will provide a more reliable indicator of a negative price change in the equity.

Figure 21 depicts, in chart format, both bullish and bearish MACD Histogram signals:

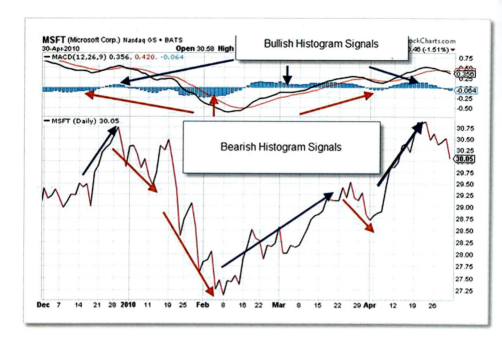

Figure 21 - MACD vs. MACD Histogram

The blue arrows, where the Histogram bars move above zero and the price of the stock rises, highlight *bullish* signals. The red arrows, where the Histogram bars move below zero and the price of the stock declines, highlight *bearish* signals. It is important to note that these histogram signals occur before the MACD itself (black line) moves above or below zero. This is why I prefer the histogram - it's a quicker indicator of change.

Summary of How to Use the MACD Histogram:

A widening gap between the MACD and its trigger line (also known as the histogram) shows strengthening momentum; a shrinking gap will demonstrate weakening momentum. A bullish signal occurs when there is positive divergence and a bullish centerline crossover. A bearish signal exists when there is negative divergence and a bearish centerline crossover. Notice, in Figure 21, how the histogram shows a bearish signal prior to the MACD (red arrows) and a bullish signal prior to the MACD (blue arrows). The histogram crosses the zero line before the MACD itself. Therefore it can be said that the *MACD and the MACD Histogram are independent of each other (Figure 21):*

Advantages of the MACD Histogram over the MACD itself:

- Divergences are apparent before MACD moving average crossovers
- Can be used to signal impending reversals
- Easy to read and quick to interpret

Conclusion - MACD

MACD and the MACD Histogram are two of the more reliable technical analysis tools available to us. They incorporate both trend-following and momentum identifying qualities and are predictive in nature. As with other technical tools, they should be used in conjunction with other indicators to assist in painting a picture for potential buy/sell decisions.

3.   *Stochastic Oscillator*

The stochastic oscillator is a momentum indicator that shows the location of the current closing price relative to the high-low range over a set number of periods, usually 14 trading days. Closing levels that are near the top of the range indicate *accumulation* or buying pressure, while those near the bottom of the range indicate *distribution* or selling pressure. Essentially the stochastic oscillator gives give you a heads up as to who is winning in the battle of the bears vs. bulls. The indicator oscillates between 0 and 100. Readings below 20 are considered *oversold* while readings above 80 are considered *overbought*. The idea behind this indicator is that *prices tend to*

Let's set up an example and see how this works. We'll assume that during the past 14 trading days, stock XYZ has seen a low of $30 and a high of $40. Today it closed at $38. Within the $10 trading range, the stock is $8 up, or "in the 80%." If the stock closed today at $32, it would be "at the 20%." This is known as %K in stochastic lingo. Transaction signals occur when %K crosses its 3-day simple moving average, called %D. %D is also known as the *trigger line*. Let's look at another chart (Figure 22) that shows the stochastic oscillator (near the bottom of the chart):

Figure 22 - Stochastic Oscillator

Note the following technical indicators shown on Figure 22:

- Stochastic Oscillator = thick black line highlighted by the black arrow = %K
- Trigger line = red line highlighted by red arrow = %D (3-d SMA)
- Overbought (80%) and oversold (20%) levels are highlighted by the green circles.

Some chartists (not me!) use crossovers of %K and %D as buy/sell signals. However, these signals occur quite frequently and can result in whipsaws, or a myriad of confusing short term signals. A more reliable reading (in my view and that of many other chartists) is when the oscillator moves from overbought (above 80%) to below that level, or from below oversold (20%) to above that level. A strong stochastic signal occurs when the positive divergence above 20% or a negative divergence below 80% takes place for a second time (i.e. a "double dip"). Here are the buy/sell signal guidelines:

Buy signal: %K crosses above the 20% for the second time

Sell signal: %K moves below the 80% for the second time.

Figure 23 shows a clear buy signal in the green encircled area, which is confirmed when the price subsequently accelerates, as shown by the green arrow on top. A definitive sell signal is also shown on this chart in the red encircled area, which is confirmed with the subsequent price decline shown by the red arrow.

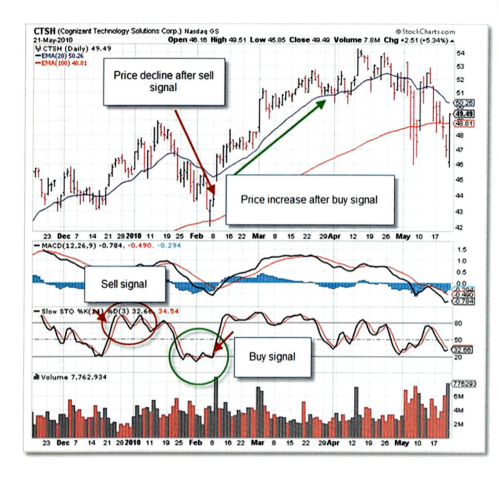

Figure 23 - Buy/Sell Signals for the Stochastic Oscillator

Slow vs. Fast Stochastics

One of the problems with %K in relation to %D is the high number of false breaks, whipsaws and crossovers. To mitigate this issue, the slow stochastic oscillator was developed, which applies a 3-day simple moving average to the %K, thereby smoothing the data to form a slower version of %K:

Slow Stochastic Oscilliator = %K (slow) = %D (fast)

To form a trigger line for this slower version, a 3-d SMA is created and applied to the new %K (slow). Therefore, the 3-d SMA of slow stochastic oscillator is the 3-d SMA of the 3-d SMA of fast stochastic oscillator (get the Tylenol!).

When building a chart, there is usually a choice of selecting slow or fast stochastics. I always opt for the slow stochastic oscillator, as it is easier to read and interpret, and eliminates many of the false triggers inherent in the fast oscillator.

Full Stochastic Oscillator

There is actually a third stochastic oscillator called full stochastics. Rather than being required to use the 3-day SMA of the %K, as in the slow stochastics, traders felt that there should be a variable so more flexibility could be achieved. A third variable was created called the *smoothing variable*, which alters the amount of days used in the smoothing of %K. One can also recreate the fast and slow stochastics by the full stochastic. To mimic the fast stochastic, use a 1-day smoothing number. To mimic the slow stochastic, use a 3-day smoothing number.

Conclusion

For purposes of short-term investing, I have found the slow stochastic oscillator most useful and time efficient. It is a widely used momentum indicator that measures who is winning the daily battle between the bulls and the bears. As always, it is prudent to use this oscillator in conjunction with our other technical indicators.

4.   Volume

Volume is the number of shares that trade over a specific period of time, usually one day. On a chart, volume is represented as a histogram (vertical bars) overlaid on or below the price chart. This indicator is an essential part of every technical formation, as a price pattern will typically have a volume pattern attached to it. In other words, we use volume to confirm trends and chart patterns. *If a stock is truly in an uptrend, we would expect the volume to be high,* which will increase the chances of the trend continuing. View this as an accelerating rocket ship with plenty of fuel to spare. Any price movement, whether up or down, with relatively high volume is seen as stronger and more reliable than a similar move on weak volume (rocket running out of fuel). The same guideline holds for changes in the MACD and stochastic oscillators. If we see positive or negative signals in these indicators, they are more significant on high volume and less so on low volume.

Some chartists will draw a *trend line* on volume and compare it to the trends of price and other technical indicators. If they are not moving in the same direction, we have a *negative volume divergence*. For example, if price is rising and volume is declining, there could be a trend reversal on the horizon. On the other hand, if price is declining and volume is accelerating, this negative trend is confirmed and a sell signal is more meaningful. Such an example can be found in Figure 24:

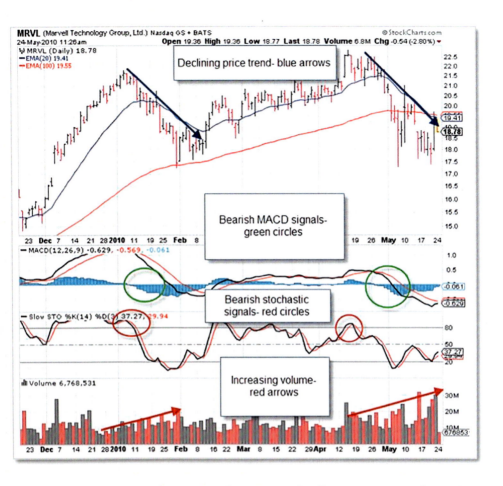

Figure 24 - Volume Confirmation of All Negative Technical Signals

Key indicators in Figure 24 include the following:

- The red arrows highlight strengthening volume
- The blue arrows show a declining price trend
- Volume is also confirming a negative MACD divergence (green circles). In other words, the green encircled area depicts a bearish moving average crossover (MACD line drops below trigger line) which is occurring on high volume (red arrows)

- Volume is also confirming a negative stochastic oscillator divergence (red circles). In other words, the red-encircled area depicts a stochastic sell signal (%K moves below the 80% in these two instances) which is occurring on high volume (red arrows).

Figure 25 depicts an example of a negative volume divergence (volume is trending in the *opposite* direction of price and other technical indicators), which, as noted, is indicative of a potential trend reversal:

Figure 25 - Volume Divergence and Trend Reversal

- Red arrows highlight volume confirmation of price acceleration
- Blue lines show weakening volume and price consolidation (sideways pattern) indicating a possible trend reversal
- The green arrow shows a severe price reversal with volume confirmation (green circle), as the volume bars during this reversal are much higher than during consolidation

Technicians who look for specific chart patterns such as triangles, flags and "head and shoulders" (not discussed in this book) can also utilize volume patterns to confirm the accuracy of those patterns.

One more quick point to remember - *volume precedes price*. If volume is weakening during an uptrend, it is oftentimes a signal that the trend is about to reverse. Note the price trend reversal as volume weakens in April in Figure 25. In April, the declining volume foreshadows a trend reversal which is confirmed by higher volume in May as the price declines.

Conclusion

Volume is an essential technical analysis tool that will verify the significance of a price pattern or technical analysis indicator confirmation or divergence. It can also be predictive of upcoming changes in chart patterns. We use volume to corroborate buy/sell signals. A positive or negative signal on high volume is much more significant than one on low volume. **Volume surges (1.5 x normal volume) are especially significant.**

Next, let's put all this information to use in a short-term trading system, see what it looks like and how to do it. First, I will show the technical parameters discussed above and then show a screenshot as to how we enter the information to create our price charts:

Constructing a Technical Chart at www.Stockcharts.com

I- Create a chart now:
   A – Style: Sharp Chart (on top of chart)
   B - Enter ticker symbol
   C - Hit "Go"

II- Chart Attributes:
   A - Periods: Daily
   B – Range: 1 year
   C – Type: OHLC Bars
   D – Size: 700 or landscape
   E – Volume: off

III - Overlays
   A - Exp Moving Average: 20
   B - Exp Moving Average: 100

IV - Indicators
   A – MACD:12, 26, 9, Below
   B - Slow Stochastics: 14, 3, Below
   C – Volume: Below

**See Figure 26 for screenshots of II, III and IV above:

Once information noted above is entered, click on "update."

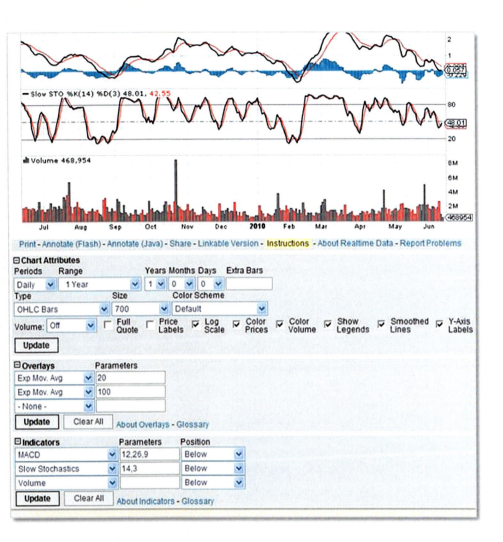

Figure 26 - Setting Up a Short-Term Technical chart

Technical Analysis and Short-Term Investing: Putting It All Together With Sample Charts

The next chart (Figure 27) shows all the short-term technical indicators discussed in this chapter. These tools allow us to make important decisions in our investment strategy. The decisions that are impacted by technical analysis are:

- Stock Selection
- Exit Strategy Determination (position management)

It is important to understand that technical analysis does not stand alone in our decision-making process. We also factor in market tone, equity fundamentals, and earnings reports and many other common sense principles.

Let's first view a chart (Figure 27) with predominantly positive, or bullish, technical indicators:

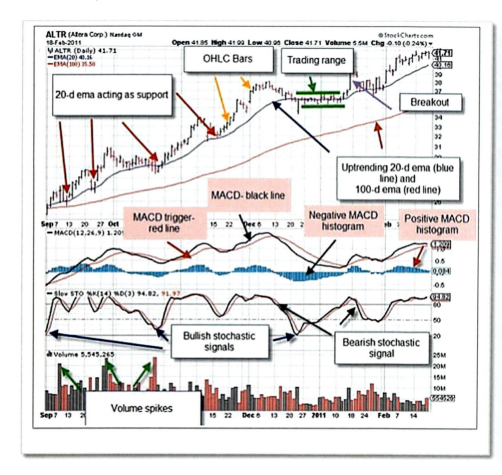

Figure 27 - Positive (Bullish) Technical

Indicators

Note, in Figure 27, the following *positive technical indicators*:

- The moving averages (red and blue lines at the top)) are uptrending as the 20-d EMA is above the 100-d EMA, both are trending higher, and the price bars are at or above the 20-d EMA.

- The MACD and its Histogram (blue bars and red arrow in middle right side of chart) are positive.

- The Stochastic Oscillator (ascending black line towards the bottom section of the chart, above volume)) has been trending up and is now above the 80% (overbought), but many equities have stayed in this territory for months.

- All these positive technical indicators have occurred on relatively strong volume (bars on the bottom of the chart).

- We are more likely to take a *bullish* stance with such a chart pattern

Figure 28, on the other hand, illustrates *mixed technical indicators*:

Figure 28 - Mixed Technical Indicators

- Moving averages (red circle at top) are uptrending, still positive and holding
- MACD is showing a bearish crossover with the trigger line, causing the histogram to move into negative territory (green circle in middle right side of chart)
- The stochastic oscillator has just completed a "double dip" below the 80%, a bearish signal (orange circle)
- These mixed signals have taken place on average to higher than average volume
- We are more likely to take a cautious approach with a chart pattern like this one

Conclusion

Technical analysis is a critical tool all investors should utilize in our investment determinations as it applies to both long and short-term investing. Chart analysis paints a picture as to what the institutional investors are doing regarding a particular security. It should be used in conjunction with each other and with other factors such as fundamental analysis, market tone, earnings report dates and others as described earlier in this book. Just as a reminder, **for purposes of our wealth-building portfolio and long-term plan, entering moving average parameters into the stock screener is all that is required regarding technical analysis.**

Wealth-Building Rules in this Chapter

- Uptrending 50-day and 200-day moving averages
- 50-day SMA above the 200-day SMA
- Stock price above the 50-day SMA

Chapter 4

Portfolio Management and Stock Selection

Chapter Outline:

- Definitions and chapter introduction
- Creating a watch list for our wealth-building portfolio
- Sample brokerage statement
- Diversification
- Asset allocation
- Common sense principles
- Portfolio rebalancing

Wealth-Building Rules in this Chapter

Our wealth-building portfolios must be diversified in the following three areas:

1. Stock
2. Industry or sector (sectors provide broader diversification than industries)
3. Cash allocation

- Never buy a stock with a trading volume lower than 500k shares per day

- Invest in a minimum of five different stocks in five different industries or sectors where no one security or group will represent more than 20%

- Allocate equal cash to each segment of our portfolios

- Portfolio rebalancing at least once a year

Definitions and chapter introduction

I am a big believer in setting yourself up for success. This is accomplished through education, motivation, commitment and *organization*. In purchasing this book, you, have already demonstrated your motivation and commitment towards educating yourself about stock market investing. However, without organization, not only will the learning process become more difficult, but the implementation process – the part where you actually start buying and selling stocks - will become much more difficult and perhaps unmanageable. With more than 7,000 stocks that trade on U.S. Exchanges, it is imperative to develop a manageable watch list of stocks from which we will make our selections. For purposes of our wealth-building portfolio, this list will be generated by our online screener (FINVIZ or one similar). As we create a watch list of the greatest performing stocks in the greatest performing industries, it becomes essential to set up organized lists of accurate information. Enter *portfolio management.*

We already know that a portfolio is a collection of financial assets such as stocks, bonds, and cash. *Portfolio management* is simply the art and science of making decisions about this investment mix, including decisions related to asset allocation, matching investment objectives to goals, entry and exit strategies and balancing risk versus returns. For purposes of our wealth-building plan, these organized lists will include:

- Stocks on our watch list, which essentially will be stocks that have passed all of our screens but have not yet made it into our portfolio (FINVIZ screener or a similar one))
- Stocks actually selected from the watch list and purchased for our wealth-building portfolio (on our brokerage statements or created by you on a spreadsheet)
- Profit/loss statements (provided by your brokerage company)

Having these organized lists will allow us to do the following in a time efficient and accurate manner:

- Select the most appropriate stocks for our portfolios
- Prepare for potential exit strategy executions (sell an underperforming stock)
- Select replacement stocks when an underperformer is sold

Creating a Watch List for Your Wealth-Building Portfolio

Figure 29 demonstrates an organized list of stocks (ticker symbols) and their current prices, generated from our FINVIZ screener. This site also has a feature where you can save a list of the stocks in your portfolio or on the watch list. Later in this chapter, we will discuss how to calculate the number of shares to purchase for our wealth-building portfolio based on the current market value of each stock in your portfolio:

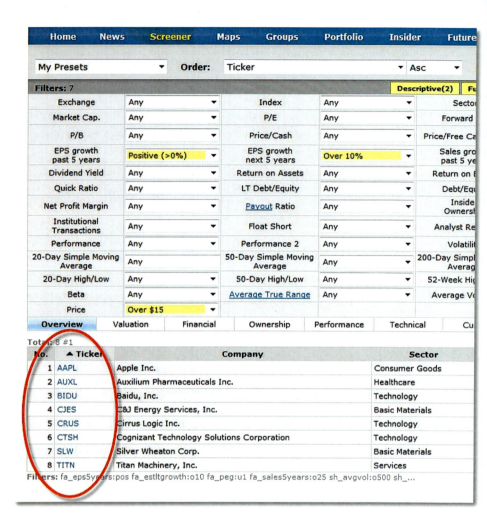

Figure 29 - Sample Watch List of Stocks or Stocks Purchased

Sample Brokerage Statement - Holdings Section

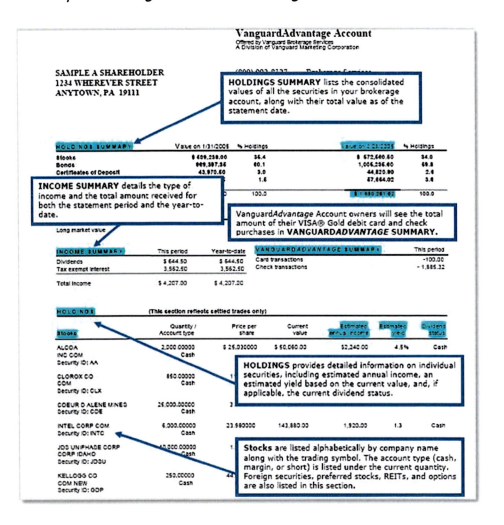

Figure 30 - Sample List of Portfolio Holdings

Brokerage statements give a lot more information than what is shown in Figure 30 (such as security values, interest and dividends and much more), and it is important to review the account summaries periodically to determine how your positions are performing.

Diversification

Diversification is a risk management technique that mixes a wide variety of investments in a portfolio. The rationale behind this strategy is that a portfolio of non-correlated investments will, on average, yield higher returns and present a lower risk than any one individual investment within that portfolio. **For our wealth-building portfolios, we must be diversified in the following three areas**:

- Stock
- Industry or sector (sectors provide broader diversification than industries)
- Cash allocation

I believe that no one stock or industry should represent more than 20% of our total stock portfolios. **Therefore, to be adequately diversified we must invest in *at least* five different stocks in five different industries or sectors with similar cash allocation (discussed shortly).** In our wealth-building portfolio, we will initiate the plan with broad-market mutual funds or exchange-traded funds (which give us automatic diversification) and move into individual stocks once we achieve a portfolio value of $25,000 (after a few years) so we can be appropriately diversified.

Asset Allocation

Asset allocation aims to balance risk and reward by dividing a portfolio's assets according to an individual's goals, risk tolerance and investment horizon. Each of the three main asset classes - stocks, fixed-income (bonds) and cash and equivalents – have different levels of risk and return, and so each asset class will behave differently over time. Asset allocation is one of the most important decisions that investors make. Here is an example of how we can divide all of the assets (not just the stock portion) in our wealth-building portfolio among the different asset classes pertaining to a high school or college age student as the portfolio size grows:

- Stocks/Mutual funds
- Bonds
- Real estate (your home is a real estate investment)
- Bank savings accounts

As an example, <u>outside of your personal residence</u> you may allocate your total portfolio as follows (just an example):

- Stocks: 80%
- Bonds: 10%
- Cash equivalents (savings): 10%

As you get older and closer to achieving your wealth-building plan you should start to consider a heavier presence in bonds and fixed income securities and perhaps this will be the topic for another book. *This book focuses on the stock portion of your portfolio, however it is important over the long haul not to neglect the other asset classes.*

Common Sense Principles

Thus far we have factored in fundamentals, technical indicators, and organized lists. This is the foundation for our stock selection process. There are, however, three more critical considerations we must consider when making our final decisions, which I call "common sense principles." Our three commons sense principles are as follows:

1.   *Minimum Trading Volume (common sense principle 1)*

Since some stocks with very low daily trading volume can be easily manipulated and may also have wide bid-ask spreads (buy/sell quotes), our common sense rule is to **never buy a stock with a trading volume lower than 500k shares per day.**

2.   *Stock and Industry Diversification (common sense principle 2)*

Investing a high percentage of your cash into one stock or industry is risky if that security or group falls out of favor with the institutional investors. By diversifying, as much as possible, with non-correlated underlying securities, we will be reducing this risk. The common sense rule is **to invest in a minimum of five different stocks in five different industries or sectors where no one security or group will represent more than 20% of your portfolio.** A way of circumventing this issue is to invest in mutual funds or exchange-traded funds, topics to be addressed in the next chapter

3.   *Cash Allocation (common sense principle 3)*

In addition to stock and industry diversification, we must also **allocate equal cash to each segment of our portfolios.** For example, if we have five stocks in our portfolio, it wouldn't make sense to have 100 shares of a $15 stock, and 100 shares of a $150 stock. To carefully balance our portfolios by cash, we will take the following steps:

- Determine how many stocks will fit your portfolio needs. A $50k portfolio will typically be best suited for about five stocks, allocating about $10k per security.
- Divide the current price per share into the amount allocated per stock and round off to the whole number.

Figure 31 demonstrates how this cash allocation breaks down for a hypothetical $50k portfolio:

A	B	C	D	E	F	G
	STOCK		PRICE		# Shares/$10k	
	A		$10		1000	
	B		$20		500	
	C		$30		333	
	D		$50		200	
	E		$100		100	

Figure 31 - Cash Allocation at about $10k per Stock

Portfolio Rebalancing

Once a year, we should look at our holdings to make sure they are properly balanced, as shown in Figure 31. If any of our holdings have dramatically risen in price, it may have a dominant impact on our stock portfolio if the price declines. Rebalancing is usually done at the end of the calendar year and involves buying or selling assets in your portfolio to maintain your original desired level of asset allocation. Those

111

with larger portfolios may want to rebalance more than once a year. For example, if at the end of the year, *stock A* represents 30% of our portfolio and *stock B* represents 10% of our portfolio, we may want to sell some shares of stock A and purchase some shares of stock B so they both then represent 20% of our overall stock portfolio.

Let's take a deep breath and summarize what we have accomplished thus far:

- Developed a method to create a watch list of the greatest performing stocks in the greatest performing industries (FINVIZ screener was shown)
- Placed our securities in an organized list in our portfolio manager (online screener portfolio, spreadsheet or brokerage statement)
- Determined which stocks to purchase (the screener was shown and will be discussed in more detail later in this book), and the number of shares per equity to purchase, using fundamental and technical analysis, as well as common sense principles. This will be addressed and detailed in Chapter 6, *Game Plan*.

Summary of wealth-building rules in Chapter 4

Our wealth-building portfolios must be diversified in the following three areas:

- Never buy a stock with a trading volume lower than 500k per day

- Invest in a minimum of five different stocks in five different industries or sectors where no one security or group will represent more than 20%

- Allocate equal cash to each segment of our portfolios

- Portfolio rebalancing at least once a year

Chapter 5

Exchange-Traded Funds, Mutual Funds and Indexes

Chapter outline:

- Exchange-Traded Funds
- Mutual Funds
- Comparing Exchange-Traded Funds and Mutual Funds

Wealth-building portfolio rule requirements in this chapter

- As we begin our journey to financial independence, we will use ETFs _or_ mutual funds to build our well-diversified portfolios until there is enough cash value to switch to individual equities and still be adequately diversified. The screening process (descriptive, fundamental, technical etc.) applies to the stock portion of our plan only and not the initial stages where we will use these broad-market exchange-traded funds or mutual funds.

Exchange Traded Funds (ETFs)

Definition and introduction

As discussed in Chapter 4, a critical requirement of our system is to be properly diversified by stock, industry and cash allocation. No one stock or industry should represent more than

20% of your portfolio holdings. One way of developing instant diversification with minimal cash outlay is to invest with exchange-traded funds or mutual funds, which are represented by baskets of stocks per unit of security. An *exchange-traded fund (ETF)* is a security that tracks an index, a commodity or a basket of assets like an index fund, but trades like a stock on an exchange. Thus, ETFs experience price changes throughout the day as it is bought and sold, and provide the diversification of an index fund. **As we begin our journey to financial independence, we will use ETFs _or_ mutual funds to build our well-diversified portfolios until there is enough cash value to switch to individual equities and still be adequately diversified.**

Who should use ETFs?

Investors with limited cash to invest, low risk tolerance or time restrictions should consider ETFs.

Advantages and disadvantages of ETFs

Investing with ETFs has several *advantages* over investing with individual securities, including:

- *Broad diversification* - By definition, an ETF inherently provides diversification across an entire index
- *Lower costs* - Many ETFs are not actively managed, thereby decreasing marketing, distribution and accounting expenses. In addition, most do not have 12b-1 fees (advertising and distribution fees).
- *Tax efficiency* - ETFs have low capital gains because of the low turnover in their portfolios.
- *No need for a financial advisor* - Why pay 1 1/2-2% a year to do something you can manage yourself?

- *Buying and selling flexibility* – ETFs maintain all the features of a stock, such as limit orders, short selling, stop orders and options.

However, ETFs have some *disadvantages*:

- *Low trading volume*
- *Limited international exposure*
- *Large bid-ask spreads or unfavorable pricing in some cases*
- *Lower dividends than individual stocks*

Bloomberg provides an excellent ETF screener based on specific criteria you select at this link:

http://www.bloomberg.com/apps/data?pid=etfscreener

Types of ETFs

Most ETFs are index funds, which are the ones that I suggest you focus on for your wealth-building portfolio. Five of the more popular ETFs on heavily traded indexes include the following:

- *QQQ* - follows a basket of 100 of the largest non-financial equities on the Nasdaq exchange.
- *VTI* - Vanguards security that tracks the total stock market.
- *VV* - Vanguards security that tracks the large cap universe
- *SCHB* - Charles Schwab multi-cap (like total stock market)
- *SCHX* - Charles Schwab large cap (like S&P 500)

Major Issuers of ETFs

- Barclays Global Investors issues iShares
- State Street Global Advisors issues street Tracks and SPDRs
- Vanguard issues Vanguard ETFs, formerly known as VIPERs.
- Merrill Lynch issues HOLDRs.
- PowerShares issuers ETFs and BLDRS (based on American Depository
- Charles Schwab

Constructing a Portfolio Using ETFs

Because ETFs inherently have instant diversification, we can purchase securities that track large segments of the overall market, or the entire market, for that matter. For example, we can purchase shares of SCHB or SCHX on a regular basis which will require very little time or effort and still be well represented in the overall market. We'll get into more details in Chapter 6, *The Game Plan*.

Mutual Funds

Overview of Mutual Funds

A *mutual fund* is a type of professionally-managed investment vehicle that collects money from many investors to purchase securities. Mutual funds are operated by money managers, who invest the fund's capital hoping to produce capital gains and income for the fund's investors. A mutual fund's portfolio is structured and maintained to match the investment objectives stated in its prospectus.

There are three types of U.S. mutual funds: *open-end*, *unit investment trust*, and *closed-end*. The open-end mutual fund, which is the most common of the three, must agree to buy back its shares from its investors at the end of every business day. ETFs (discussed above) are open-end funds, or unit investment trusts, that trade on national securities exchanges such as the NYSE and NASDAQ.

Mutual funds are classified by their principal investments. The four largest categories of funds are money market funds, bond or fixed income funds, *stock funds* (our main focus) and hybrid funds. Funds may also be categorized as index (passive) or actively-managed.

Advantages and Disadvantages of Mutual Funds

Investing with mutual funds has several *advantages* over investing with individual stocks, including:

- Increased diversification
- Daily liquidity
- Professional investment management
- Ability to participate in investments that may be available only to larger investors
- Service and convenience
- Government oversight
- Ease of comparison
- Ability to be purchased by dollar amount rather than whole share amount

However, mutual funds do have *disadvantages*:

- Fees (in some instances)
- Less control over timing of recognition of gains
- Less predictable income

- No opportunity to customize

Types of Mutual Funds

As noted above, there are three types of U.S. mutual funds: (1) *open-end*; (2) *unit investment trust*, and (3) *closed-end*. The following discussion addresses each of these mutual funds in turn:

Open-end Funds

Open-end mutual funds must be willing to buy back their shares from their investors at the end of every business day at the *net asset value (NAV)* computed that day. NAV per share is based on the closing market prices of the securities in the fund's portfolio. All mutual funds' buy and sell orders are processed at the NAV of the trade date. However, investors must wait until the following day to get the trade price.

Most open-end funds also sell shares to the public every business day; these shares are also priced at net asset value. A professional investment manager oversees the portfolio. The total investment in the fund will vary based on share purchases, share redemptions and fluctuation in market valuation. There is no legal limit on the number of shares that can be issued. *This is the most common form of a mutual fund.*

Closed-End Funds

Closed-end funds issue shares to the public only once – when they are created through an *initial public offering (IPO)*. Their shares are then listed for trading on a national securities exchange such as the NYSE or NASDAQ. Investors who no longer wish to invest in the fund cannot sell their shares back to the fund (as they can with an open-end fund). Instead, they must sell their shares to another investor in the secondary market; the price they receive may be different from net asset value. It may be at a "premium" to net asset value (meaning that it is higher than net asset value) or more commonly, at a "discount" to net asset value (meaning that it is lower than net asset value). A professional investment manager oversees the portfolio. *Closed-end funds are much less popular than the open-end funds.*

Unit Investment Trusts

Unit investment trusts, or UITs, issue shares to the public only once, when they are created. Investors can redeem shares directly with the fund (as with an open-end fund), or they may also be able to sell their shares in the market. *Unit investment trusts do not have a professional investment manager.* UITs offer a fixed, unmanaged portfolio, generally of stocks and bonds, as redeemable *units* to investors for a specified time frame. It is designed to provide capital appreciation and/or dividend income.

Comparing ETFs and Mutual Funds

The exchange-traded fund or ETF is often structured as an open-end investment company. ETFs combine characteristics of both closed-end funds and open-end funds. Like closed-end funds, ETFs are traded throughout the day on a stock exchange at a price determined by the market. However, as with open-end funds, investors normally receive a price that is close to net asset value. To keep the market price close to net asset value, ETFs issue and redeem large blocks of their shares with institutional investors. *ETFs are becoming more and more popular as of the penning of this book in late 2013.*

ETFs	Mutual Funds
Pricing throughout the day	Price set after market close
Traded on exchanges	Redeemed by fund
Can control tax liability	Little control over tax liability
Limit orders and shorting allowed	No limit orders or shorting
Brokerage commissions apply	No-load funds-no transaction fees
Purchased in any brokerage	Availability limited
Lower expense ratios	Higher expenses due to sales loads
Margin permitted (I don't advise this)	No margin allowed
No tax impact from broker trading	May be capital gains distributions

Figure 32 - ETFs v Mutual Funds

ETFs and mutual funds are critical investment vehicles that will allow us kick-start our wealth-building portfolios with minimal cash investments while still providing sufficient diversification at relatively low trading costs.

In Chapter 6 we will put all the information detailed thus far into action in order to establish our wealth-building game plan.

Chapter 6

The Game Plan

Chapter Outline:

- Game plan assumptions
- Estimating growth of your wealth-building portfolio/ Using a Compound Savings Calculator
- Getting started by saving $1000.00
- Opening your first brokerage account with mutual funds
- Dollar cost averaging (DCA)
- Moving from mutual funds to stocks
- Sample initial portfolio using a stock screener
- Expanding the number of stocks in an appreciating portfolio
- Stock investing (step 3) summary

Wealth-Building Rules in this Chapter

- Write down your goal and place it where it can be seen every day
- Favor mutual funds for our initial investments
- Favor the Schwab or Vanguard family of mutual funds
- Instruct your broker to re-invest all dividend distributions
- Use dollar cost averaging and auto-withdrawal to simplify the process
- Move from mutual funds to stocks when portfolio value reaches $25,000.00

I am a firm believer in the notion that any investment-related game plan must be realistic to be successful. A brief analogy is instructive in this regard: if a friend asked me for advice on how to lose weight, I would advise a lifestyle change of diet and exercise that involves a *gradual* shift from his or her current status (I am also a certified personal fitness trainer). Suggesting a starvation diet of 1,000 calories per day would not work in the long run. If my buddy was a couch potato, a plan of going to the gym five days a week for two hours of cardio and weight training is not a reasonable short-term goal. Instead, I would help my friend develop a sensible plan that is achievable – one that can be *gradually* enhanced and developed. The same approach applies to our wealth-building strategy. Our investment game plan must be based on sound fundamental, technical and common sense principles, and our execution of this game plan must be time efficient and easy to implement.

Game Plan Assumptions

With these thoughts in mind, prior to delving into the investment strategy for our wealth-building portfolio, I will make certain assumptions that will have broad application. **You can adjust your plan based on your specific situation, so do not worry if these assumptions are not directly applicable to you.** Here are the assumptions that will be used as we move forward:

- You are starting to invest at age 18, with a goal of retiring a millionaire by age 58
- You have little or no money to start, but can manage to save $1,000 to initiate this journey

- You will invest 10% of your gross annual income in your wealth-building portfolio (e.g. earn $60,000, invest $500/month, or $6,000 annually)
- You will **average** an annual gross income of $60,000 for the first 20 years (invest $500/month into portfolio), and $80,000 for the last 20 years of our 40-year program (invest $666.00/per month)
- We will use an annual return of 8%, the lower end of the stock market's historical returns, as discussed earlier in this book. This will represent a minimum projected return but we will set up our strategy to achieve even higher long-term results (moving to individual stocks)
- The preceding and ensuing stats are per-family income earner

Estimating Your Wealth-Building Portfolio Growth/Using A Compound Savings Calculator

The first step in setting ourselves up for success is to **write down on paper our reasonable long-term goals. $1.8 million by age 58 if you start at age 18 (adjust according to the age you will begin).** Write it down! Then place it in an area where you will view it every day, perhaps adjacent to your computer. Using the assumptions stated above, we can calculate the estimated growth of our wealth-building portfolio <u>for the first 20 years</u> using a free online *compound savings calculator [bankrate.com is one such site]* which takes a lump sum of money ($1,000 to start) and compounds it (generates investment profits from prior investment profits) over a fixed period of time, and at a fixed annual yield (we will use 8%). In addition to the initial investment it allows you to add monthly contributions and compound those as well.

Figure 33 illustrates the value of your wealth-building portfolio based on the aforementioned assumptions:

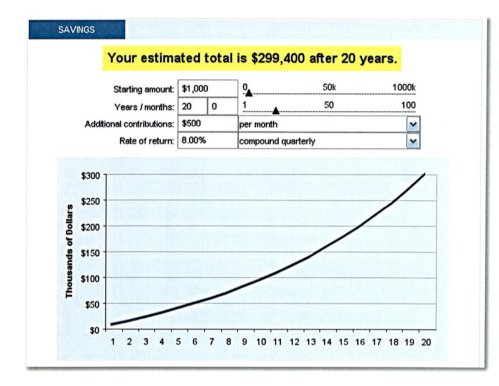

Figure 33 - Estimated Growth of Your Wealth Building Portfolio Over 20 Years (Source: Bankrate.com)

As Figure 33 demonstrates, at the end 20 years our wealth-building portfolio would boast an estimated cash value of $299,400, assuming an initial investment of $1,000 and $500 monthly contributions with an 8% annual return compounded quarterly. But the fun is just beginning! For the second 20 years of our 40-year program, we will average (based on the initial assumptions) an annual gross income of $80,000, and thus will invest $8,000 annually into our wealth-building portfolio, which translates into $666.00/month (10% of our annual income).

126

Let's go to Figure 34 and see how much money our wealth-building portfolio is estimated to have after 40 years:

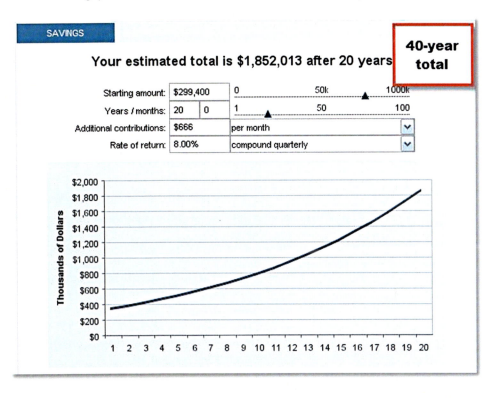

Figure 34 - Estimated Growth of Your Wealth Building Portfolio Over 40 Years

As Figure 34 illustrates, at the end of 40 years, our wealth-building portfolio boasts a whopping estimated cash value of $1,852,013 using the stated assumptions!

Our goal is now set. Don't forget to write it down. Our mission is to use our long-term investment plan to retire a millionaire at a relatively young age (age 58 if one starts at age 18. Yes, 58 is a relatively young in the context of retirement!). If your family consists of two income earners, you can adjust your goal accordingly. You may opt to retire at a younger age, at the same age with more cash, or use the same goal with a lower monthly percentage of investment (per total income). This is a *realistic* goal based on sound fundamental, technical and common sense principles. *The key is to take advantage of your youth and start at a young age. Start now* (well not at this very minute, but you know what I mean). Don't let this incredible, once-in-a-lifetime opportunity pass you by as I did!

Step 1: Getting Started By Saving $1,000

To achieve our goal, we will need to raise our initial capital of $1,000. Let me first state the obvious. **As a student in high school or college, your primary focus is on your education.** That is of utmost importance. When you seek a part-time job, it should be one that allows you to manage both aspects of your primary goals – your education and beginning your investment career. When special occasions such as birthdays or your graduation arise, make sure friends and family know how much you would appreciate stocks rather than that new video game. They will provide the cash, and you will make the non-emotional, informed selections. You may develop other innovative ways of generating additional income. For example, when I was in college, one of my friends went to local businesses to sell advertising space on a desk blotter that had yet to be designed. He pocketed over $1,500 for two months of time and effort...not bad! Use your imagination as you take a look at that note posted next to your computer . . . $1.8 million by age 58!

Step 2: Opening Your First Brokerage Account With Mutual Funds

Once you have accumulated your $1,000 initial investment cash, it's time to open your first brokerage account, which you must have if you want to buy and sell securities. Congratulations on this landmark accomplishment! I'll bet your family will be proud of you, and your friends will wonder what's going on with their pal. In the next chapter, we will discuss the various types of accounts available to you. For now, let's assume your account is open and ready for action. Since the capital available at this point is not adequate to support individual equities (stocks) while still being properly diversified, we will consider mutual funds or ETFs. I particularly like the Vanguard (www.vanguard.com) and Charles Schwab (www.schwab.com) families of funds because of the low expense ratios (administrative fees) associated with their products.

Our decision to use a mutual index fund (that is based on a broad market index such as the S&P 500 or the Total Stock Market), or an ETF (which would also be based on a broad market index), depends on the cost to trade and the fund expenses since the investment returns will otherwise be similar. In other words, we must figure out which ETF or mutual fund will cost us the least and be most practical to use. Ideally, we would use mutual funds in a tax-sheltered account such as an Investment Retirement Account (IRA), since there will be no commissions or tax consequences from capital gains distributions. In addition, when investing in ETFs, trading commissions (percentage wise) are much greater at the beginning because we are investing less cash now than we will be in the future. This means that an $8 commission on a monthly investment of $100 has a more deleterious effect on your portfolio (percentage wise) than does an $8 commission on an investment of $600. Some brokerages (such as Charles Schwab) do not charge commission if you invest in *their* mutual funds or ETFs. **In general, we will favor mutual funds over ETFs when we open our brokerage accounts for the following reason:**

Mutual fund shares can be purchased via automatic withdrawal in dollar rather than share amounts so there is very little time and effort required once we have the account set up. For example, we can set up an account where $100 worth of a broad market mutual fund is purchased on the 1st of every month.

Over the years, I have favored the Vanguard family of funds because of their low expense ratios (fees they charge to manage these funds). However, Charles Schwab has caught up with (and even surpassed) these low administrative costs. In addition, Vanguard requires a higher initial investment ($3000.00) to open an account than does Schwab ($100.00). *With Schwab, you can open an account with $1000.00 or with an automatic monthly purchase plan of $100.00 or more.* **Therefore, we will look to the Charles Schwab family of mutual index funds.** Figure 35 details two great choices of Schwab Equity Index Funds:

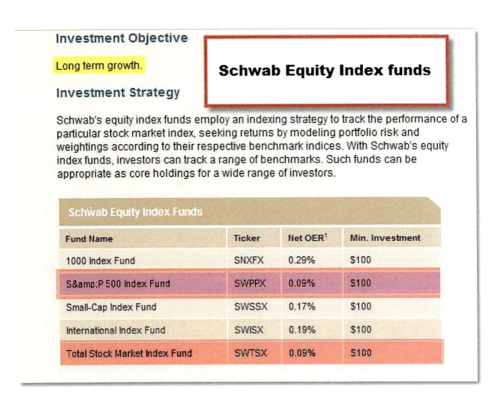

Investment Objective

Long term growth.

Investment Strategy

Schwab Equity Index funds

Schwab's equity index funds employ an indexing strategy to track the performance of a particular stock market index, seeking returns by modeling portfolio risk and weightings according to their respective benchmark indices. With Schwab's equity index funds, investors can track a range of benchmarks. Such funds can be appropriate as core holdings for a wide range of investors.

Schwab Equity Index Funds

Fund Name	Ticker	Net OER[1]	Min. Investment
1000 Index Fund	SNXFX	0.29%	$100
S&P 500 Index Fund	SWPPX	0.09%	$100
Small-Cap Index Fund	SWSSX	0.17%	$100
International Index Fund	SWISX	0.19%	$100
Total Stock Market Index Fund	SWTSX	0.09%	$100

Figure 35 - Charles Schwab Equity Index Funds

Note how both the Schwab Total Stock Market (SWTSX) and S&P 500 (SWPPX) Index funds have the following two favorable traits:

- Extremely low expense ratios of 0.09% (about half that of Vanguard's low rates)

- Low minimum investment requirement of $100

Dollar Cost Averaging (DCA)

In step 2, we opened our brokerage account with the $1,000 in cash earned through hard work, gifts and innovative ideas.

131

At this point we continue to invest (as we will over the next 40 years) using a strategy called *dollar cost averaging (DCA)*. Each year we estimate what our annual gross income will be and plan to invest 10% of that amount. Each month we invest one twelfth of that figure. Our assumption is that over the first 20 years of our wealth-building plan, we will average $60,000 per year. DCA is a technique of buying a fixed dollar amount of a particular investment on a regular schedule, regardless of the share price. More shares are purchased when prices are low, and fewer shares are bought when prices are high. For example, if your early income is $12,000 per year (about $230 per week from work and gifts), your goal is to invest $1,200 per year, or $100 per month. If the net asset value (NAV) of each fund unit is $10, your monthly investment of $100 will buy 10 shares or units. If the price increases to $20 per share, you will purchase 5 shares and so on. In the long run, you will own more shares at a lower price and this technique will protect you from dramatic share (market) depreciation. You can make the process even simpler by setting up an automatic purchase on a specific time of the month. If you get paid every two weeks, plan to purchase the fund after the second check arrives. Set up a *dollar amount*, not a share amount. *Mutual fund units can be purchased fractionally.* For example, if the per unit price of a mutual fund is $12, an investment of $100 will purchase 8.33 shares. Additionally, when filling out the brokerage account form, **check the box that instructs your broker to re-invest all dividend distributions.** Many stocks generate dividends which are usually distributed quarterly. We want this cash to get reinvested to purchase additional shares, even if fractional shares. This will represent an additional, significant income stream into your wealth-building portfolio.

Step 3: Moving From Mutual Funds To Stocks When Account Value Reaches $25,000.00

As we approach our stage 2 goal of achieving a portfolio net worth of $25,000, it's time to turn to individual equities. You can use the same brokerage account originally set up for mutual funds. Utilizing carefully selected stocks that meet our fundamental, technical and common sense screens will allow us to generate higher returns than broad market index mutual funds while still remaining properly diversified. We now re-visit our FINVIZ stock screener (or a similar one) using the criteria set up in the earlier chapters. We select 5 different stocks in 5 different sectors or industries and place them in a portfolio manager watch list. We will keep in mind our rule regarding cash allocation where no one stock or industry will have a cash value much higher or lower than the others. Each equity will represent approximately $5000.00 of our stage 3 portfolio initially (one fifth of $25,000.00). Five months prior to reaching our $25,000 goal, we will begin to dollar cost average into each of the 5 stocks. Each month we will invest $1000.00 into each of the 5 securities. As we take this action, we continue to deposit 10% of our gross annual income into our mutual fund account. Bear in mind that we always want to keep enough cash value in the mutual fund account to keep it open as this account will "feed" our stock portfolio. At the end of this 5-month time frame our stock portfolio will contain approximately $5,000.00 of each of the 5 equities depending on price movement over that time frame. There will also be a few thousand dollars of cash value in our mutual fund account. Each month we continue to invest into our mutual fund account as we have for years. When the cash value is at least $5,000.00 + additional value to keep the account open, we transfer $5000.00 into our stock account and purchase $1,000 worth of each of our 5 stocks.

From a wealth-accumulation perspective, here is our 3-step approach, which is also illustrated in Figure 36):

- Save $1000.00 using work income, gifts and innovative ideas to open your first brokerage account

- $1,000.00 - $25,000.00: Dollar cost average into a Charles Schwab broad market index mutual fund

- $25,000.00 - $1.8 million: Dollar cost average into individual equities using appropriate exit strategies and portfolio rebalancing

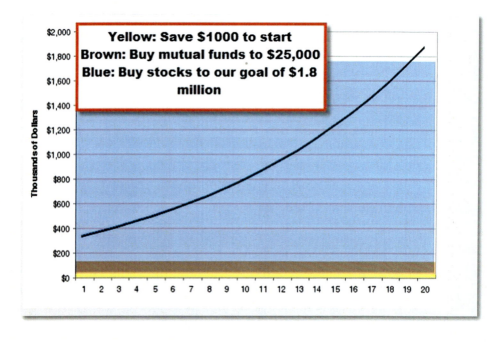

Figure 36 –The 3 Stages of Meeting Our Goal of $1.8 Million

Once we have achieved our stage 2 goal of reaching a portfolio net worth of $25,000 (start 5 months prior to achieving this goal), we now turn to our stock screener to create a watch list of individual stocks. We use the descriptive, fundamental and technical criteria detailed earlier in this book. Here is a sample initial portfolio:

Sample initial portfolio using the stock screener

▲ Ticker	Company	Sector	Industry	Country	Market Cap	P/E	Price
AGCO	AGCO Corporation	Industrial Goods	Farm & Construction Machinery	USA	4.48B	6.45	46.15
ATW	Atwood Oceanics, Inc.	Basic Materials	Oil & Gas Drilling & Exploration	USA	3.01B	11.11	46.00
BVN	Compania de Minas Buenaventura SA	Basic Materials	Gold	Peru	9.03B	10.78	32.77
DFS	Discover Financial Services	Financial	Credit Services	USA	21.00B	9.63	41.61
GES	Guess' Inc.	Services	Apparel Stores	USA	2.20B	10.19	25.87
GMCR	Green Mountain Coffee Roasters Inc.	Consumer Goods	Processed & Packaged Goods	USA	5.70B	16.90	36.67
HAL	Halliburton Company	Basic Materials	Oil & Gas Equipment & Services	USA	30.95B	10.65	33.35
JOY	Joy Global, Inc.	Industrial Goods	Farm & Construction Machinery	USA	6.03B	8.12	56.99
NTES	NetEase.com, Inc.	Technology	Internet Software & Services	China	5.74B	10.18	43.86
OIS	Oil States International Inc.	Basic Materials	Oil & Gas Equipment & Services	USA	3.88B	8.81	70.72
PAY	VeriFone Systems, Inc	Consumer Goods	Business Equipment	USA	3.28B	13.94	30.39
UHS	Universal Health Services Inc.	Healthcare	Hospitals	USA	4.38B	10.94	45.07
UTHR	United Therapeutics Corporation	Healthcare	Drug Manufacturers - Other	USA	2.67B	10.81	52.55

Figure 37 - Sample Portfolio

Our strict screening requirements deliver a watch list as shown in Figure 37. Note the following:

- Four of the sectors have more than one candidate

- We will select no more than one stock from each sector

- We will select a total of 5 stocks in 5 different sectors

- In this <u>sample</u> portfolio, the selected stocks are highlighted in light blue (other stocks from the watch list could have been chosen)

- We will allocate approximately $5,000 per stock by dividing the price-per-share into $5,000

Here is what our sample initial portfolio may look like after dollar-cost-averaging into our securities <u>over a 5-month period</u> (Figure 38):

	A	B	C	D	E	F	G	H
	<u>STOCK</u>		<u>PRICE/SHARE</u>		<u># SHARES/$5,000</u>		<u>TOTAL COST</u>	
	ATW		$46		108		$4,968	
	DFS		$41.61		120		$4,993	
	GMCR		$36.67		136		$4,987	
	JOY		$56.99		88		$5,015	
	UHS		$45.07		111		$5,002	
					<u>TOTAL</u>		$24,965	

Figure 38 - Sample Portfolio by # of Shares and Cost per Position

Expanding the number of stocks in our appreciating portfolio

As the cash value of your wealth-building portfolio increases you can further diversify by increasing the number of stocks you own. Here are some *guidelines*:

Portfolio value	Number of stocks
$100k	up to 10 stocks ($10k per equity)
$200k	up to 15 stocks ($13k per equity)
$300k and higher	up to 20 stocks ($15k per equity) (Cap at 20 stocks)
$500k	up to 20 stocks ($25k per equity)
$1,500,000	up to 20 stocks ($75k per equity)

Here is a summary of our step 3 activity which **begins 5 months before reaching our $25,000.00 goal**:

Step 3 summary

- Set up a watch list of 5 stocks in 5 different industries using the FINVIZ (or similar) stock screener
- Purchase approximately $1000.00 of each equity at the same time of the month for the next 5 months
- Continue to invest one twelfth of 10% of your gross annual income into your mutual fund account each month

- When the mutual fund account builds up to $5000.00 + transfer $5,000.00 into your stock account *making sure enough cash value remains to keep the mutual fund account open*
- Continue to purchase $1000.00 of each stock when cash is available
- Increase the number of stocks in your portfolio as its cash value increases

***See Appendix VII for alternate time frames demonstrating that the earlier you get started, the easier and more meaningful your investments will impact your life.

Wealth-Building Rules in this Chapter

- Write down your goal and place it where it can be seen every day
- Favor mutual funds for our initial investments
- Favor the Schwab or Vanguard family of mutual funds
- Instruct your broker to re-invest all dividend distributions
- Use dollar cost averaging and auto-withdrawal to simplify the process
- Move from mutual funds to stocks when portfolio value reaches $25,000.00

In the next chapter, we will discuss how to execute our trades and manage our positions.

Chapter 7

Executing and Managing
Our Stock Trades

Chapter Outline: Executing stock trades

- Order types
- Trade execution form
- Additional customer orders
- Brokerage accounts
- Customer account ownership
- Custodial accounts

Chapter Outline: Managing Stock Trades

- Trailing stop loss order
- Management summary

Wealth-Building Rules in this Chapter

- Make sure your brokerage trading platform has the ability to accept trailing stop orders
- We will use a 10% trailing stop loss order on each position
- Use an online discount broker
- Open a cash account, not a margin account

Executing Our Stock Trades

Before purchasing our first equity shares, we must become familiar with the order types available to us, and the online brokerage firms that will provide the platform that will allow us to buy and sell our stocks. We must also become familiar with the broker trade execution form to ensure that each section is filled out properly. Let's first start with the three most common customer orders types used to execute equity transactions as it relates to our wealth-building plan.

Order Types

Market Order - An order that an investor makes through a broker to buy or sell a stock (or option) immediately at the <u>best available current price</u>. Market orders are the default choice for most brokerage firms, and are likely to be executed in full because these orders do not contain any price restrictions. Since almost all our candidates are highly liquid (trade a significant number of shares per day), market orders are appropriate for our wealth-building portfolios

Limit Order - An order placed with a brokerage to buy or sell a set number of shares <u>at a specified price or better</u>. Limit orders also allow an investor to limit the length of time an order can be outstanding before being cancelled. Depending on the direction of the position, limit orders are sometimes referred to more specifically as a buy limit order, or a sell limit order. A buy limit order can be set at a specific price or better (lower). Personally, I use limit orders when trading stock options, a topic I will discuss in the latter part of this book.

Trailing Stop Loss Order – This is an instruction to our broker to sell our shares if the price drops to a certain level. A stop-loss order is set at a percentage level below the market price (we will employ a 10% figure) for a long stock position. The trailing stop price is adjusted as the price fluctuates. If we buy a stock for $30 and place a 10% trailing stop loss order, we are instructing our broker to sell if the price drops to $27 or lower. If share price appreciates higher than $30, the 10% stop loss order will be reset at a higher price (but never at a lower price). The trailing stop order can be placed as a trailing stop limit order, or a trailing stop market order. **Make sure your brokerage trading platform has the ability to accept trailing stop orders**. Use a "Good Till Cancelled" (GTC) order (not a day order), and make sure you know if this order will expire. Different brokerages have different rules in this regard. For example, a GTC order at Schwab lasts for 60 calendar days. With some brokerages you can also use a *bracket order* that will not expire unless cancelled or filled. This is the best choice for our plan (if GTC does expire). If not, a GTC order will have to be placed again at the end of the active period (60 days at Schwab and can vary with other brokerages).

Trade Execution Form:
Placing An Online Order To Buy Or Sell A Security

In order to buy or sell a stock or mutual fund online, you will need to fill out a trading form to instruct your broker what you want accomplished. In Figure 39, let's look at a sample brokerage trade execution form and the main areas to focus on. This screenshot was taken from the Charles Schwab web site and is typical of the forms you will find on most online discount brokerages sites you may consider:

Figure 39 - Trade Execution Form (Charles Schwab)

Trade Execution Form Highlights (Figure 39)

- Row 1: Cash balance

- Row 2: Ticker symbol/ current price

- Row 3: Stocks & ETFs category

- Row 4: Action (buy); Quantity; Order Type; Limit Price; Timing

- Row 5: Review Order (before executing trade)

- Row 6: Trailing Stop Exit (10%)

The trade execution form is located in the "Stocks and ETFs" section of the brokerage site and shown in the screenshot (row 3). We first confirm that the account has enough available cash to execute our intended trades. By entering the ticker symbols of the stocks we will purchase, we can see the most recent market price. If all this information meets with your approval, it's time to enter your instructions:

- Enter the number of shares

- Enter market or limit order (market will usually suffice)

- Enter timing (day only)

- Enter trailing stop loss order of 10% (GTC or " bracket" order)

- Review trade order before executing trade

Once you have confirmed that your order has been executed (usually in seconds), move on to your next trade. The information provided in this chapter thus far is the meat and potatoes of what you need to know for executing trades. However, in the next section, I have included a more detailed analysis of the types of orders available to use for other trading strategies.

Additional Customer Orders

Orders that we place with our online discount broker can take several different forms, depending on our investment strategies and objectives. We can buy or sell; make an online request for a specific price or simply the best available price; stipulate an action given a particular circumstance; or use combinations of orders. Let's look at the most common orders types and the situations during which we may utilize them. I will leave out the market order, limit order and trailing stop loss order we previously discussed and the ones you will be employing the most. Here are the others:

Stop Order

An order to buy or sell a security when its price surpasses a specific price called the *stop price*. At that point the stop order becomes a *market order*. A *sell stop order* is placed below the current market value of the stock and is used to prevent or limit a loss or to protect a profit on a long stock position. For example, you may have purchased a stock for $20 per share and it has appreciated to $30. A sell stop order at $25 will guarantee at least a profit of $5 per share (barring a gap-down in the price of the stock). A *buy stop order* is always placed above the current market price of the stock. It is typically used to protect a profit or limit a loss on a short sale (selling a stock you didn't own by borrowing it from your broker). For example, if you sell short a stock at $30 (a risky strategy where you "borrow" the stock from your brokerage) expecting to buy it back at a lower price but it starts going up in value instead, a buy stop order can limit your loss. It may kick in at $32 thereby minimizing losses to $2 per share. Once the *buy stop price* is reached, the order becomes a market order.

Stop Limit Order

This is a combination of a *stop order* and a *limit order*. Once activated, it becomes a limit order which means that it can only be executed at a specific price or better. The benefit is that the trader has precise control over when the order should be filled (at the specified price). The disadvantage is that it may never get filled. A *sell stop-limit order* is always placed below the current market price of the equity and is used to limit the loss or protect the profit on a long stock position. Once activated, it

144

becomes a limit order. A *buy stop-limit order* is always placed above the current price of the stock and is used to limit a loss or protect the profit on a short stock position. Once activated, it becomes a limit order.

Day Order vs. Good 'Til Canceled (GTC) Order

A day order is an order to buy or sell a security that automatically expires if not executed on the day the order was placed. A day order is an order that is good for that day only. If it is not filled it will be canceled, and it will not be filled if the limit or stop order price was not met during the trading session. A "good till canceled (GTC)" order will remain active until it is manually canceled. We will use day orders when buying our shares and GTC orders when entering our trailing stop orders as discussed in the management section below.

One Order Cancels the Other (OCO)

One order cancels another order. This occurs when two orders are entered simultaneously with the condition that if one order is executed, the second is cancelled. This an advanced order generally reserved for experienced traders employing strategies that are more complicated than those discussed in this book.

One Order Triggers Another Order (OTO)

One order triggers another order. This is where you enter an order, and if that order is executed, another order is automatically submitted. This an advanced order generally reserved for experienced traders employing strategies that are more complicated than those discussed in this book.

Summary of Orders Entered Above the Market

- Buy Stop-Limit
- Buy Stop
- Sell Limit

Summary of Orders entered Below Market

- Buy Limit
- Sell Stop
- Sell Stop-Limit
- Trailing stop

Brokerage Accounts

Full Service vs. Discount Brokers

- *Full Service Brokers* are best suited for investors who need guidance and personalized attention. They offer direction and advice, make investment decisions on your behalf and assist you in achieving your financial goals. The main disadvantage is the higher costs associated with full service brokers and the concern that these representatives are salespeople who may not have your best interest in mind. That being said, there are many outstanding full service brokerages but for purposes of our wealth-building strategy, trading costs must be kept to a minimum so we will favor online discount brokerages (see Appendix II).
- *Discount Brokers* are best suited for investors who have a definite plan and the confidence to execute it properly without outside assistance (that's you!). They offer lower trading cost, unbiased service as well as access to educational material. **I recommend using an online**

discount broker for your journey to financial independence.

For a free broker report, contact FINRA at:

www.finra.org

301-590-6500

In Appendix II, I provide a list of several online discount brokers and their contact information.

Types of Brokerage Accounts

There are three types of brokerage accounts: cash, margin and option:

- In a *cash account*, the client must pay, in full and by the settlement date, the amount due on any transaction. All money and securities in a cash account are wholly owned by the client and entirely held in her name. **This is the type of account I recommend as you initiate your investment career.**

- A *margin account* allows the client to borrow money or securities from the broker-dealer in order to gain greater leverage on her transactions - that is, to buy as much as double what she could with a cash account. Before the account is activated, the client must sign a *hypothecation agreement* (applies to securities in a margin account used as collateral for money loaned from a brokerage). The broker-dealer must document that the client has been informed of all risks associated with trading on margin. A margin account must have at least $2,000 in invested capital; a day trader's margin account must have at least $25,000.

- An *option account* is a margin account approved by the broker-dealer for trading on the CBOE. The client will get such approval only if the broker-dealer determines that there is adequate equity in the account, that the client has adequate net worth and that the client is sophisticated enough to invest prudently in the riskier realm of options trading. A more detailed risk disclosure statement is required. In Chapter 12, there will be a discussion of *covered call writing*, a conservative options strategy that can be used to generate a second income in your portfolio. You will need an option account should you decide to take advantage of this strategy.

*** There will be a discussion of sheltered (Traditional and Roth IRA) and non-sheltered accounts in Chapter 9 concerning *Tax Implications*.

Customer Account Ownership

There are several arrangements for ownership of a customer account, and these are the two most important:

1. *Individual Account:* A simple account with the name of one, and only one, real person attached.

2. *Joint Account:* Typically used by people who are married or cohabiting. Joint accounts are almost always for two people who are residing together.

However, this is a matter of social convention rather than law, and it is not inconceivable to have joint accounts with more than two names attached. There are two categories here:

- *Joint Tenants with Right of Survivorship (JTWROS)*: Under a JTWROS account, both parties named on the account own every dime in it and each has equal rights to the property. Either owner can conduct account business on behalf of both. In the event of the death of one, the survivor automatically gets the interest of the deceased. This keeps the probate lawyers away.

- *Joint Tenants in Common (JTIC)*: Under JTIC, there is no right of survivorship, and the decedent's will stipulates how his interest will be passed to his heirs.

Custodial Accounts

An account created at a bank, brokerage firm or mutual fund company that is managed by an adult for a minor that is under the age of 18 to 21 (depending on state legislation). You may need to open this type of account depending on your age and the state you live in. This would apply to the "step 2" or mutual fund aspect of our wealth-building strategy.

Although the general principles for custodial accounts are the same across the country, the age when a child can take control of the account and assets (also called the "age of majority") varies from 18 to 21, and is sometimes even older, depending on the circumstances and the state. Be sure to ask a financial consultant about the law in your state.

Other *important details* you should consider in connection with custodial accounts include:

- Custodial accounts are simpler to establish than trusts, which generally require more planning and the help of an attorney. However, a trust can offer more flexibility, control, and protection than a custodial account.

- As of 2009, anyone can give a monetary gift of up to $13,000 (or $26,000 per couple splitting gifts) to each recipient without incurring federal gift tax. (This rule applies to custodial accounts as well as other forms of gifts.)

- As the donor, a parent or another adult may be designated to be the custodian of the account. If the donor acts as the custodian, and he or she dies before the account terminates, the account value will be included in the donor's estate for estate tax purposes.

- The custodian has sole responsibility to manage the assets for the minor until the custodianship ends, usually when the minor reaches the age of 18 or 21, depending on the state.

- All custodial assets must be used "for the use and benefit of the minor." While this may be subject to interpretation, it's clear that custodians should never use the money for expenses unrelated to the child's interests, or for day-to-day living expenses and other expenses the custodial parent or legal guardian is legally obligated to pay. If the custodian is the child's parent or legal guardian, then it's advisable to get advice from a financial consultant regarding allowed distributions before making any withdrawal from the account for the benefit of the child.

- Money and assets deposited into a custodial account immediately become property of the child. This is not revocable. In other words, you can't change your mind, take the assets back or give the assets to someone else. If circumstances arise that require a change, the custodian should seek legal advice before making any changes.

- The account must be turned over to the child once the custodianship ends. (At that time, the custodian's access to the account may be restricted.) The child will then have complete control over the account. He or she may choose to sell any investments in the account or close the account and request a check for the proceeds. Alternatively, he or she may convert the account to his or her own name, establish the custodian as a joint account holder, or grant the custodian power of attorney on the account.

- Any investment income—such as dividends, interest or earnings—generated by account assets is considered the child's income and taxed at the child's tax rate once the child reaches age 18. If the child is younger than 18, the first $950 is untaxed, and the next $950 is taxed at the child's rate. Anything over $1,900 is taxed at the parent's rate.

- Custodial accounts don't let you designate what happens to the money in the account if the child dies before receiving it (it is part of their estate and distributed according to the laws of your state). With a trust, however, you may make this decision.

Managing Our Stock Positions

Trailing stop loss order

Despite the system's meticulous screening process our stock positions can depreciate in value for a myriad of reasons. Years ago, companies like Bear Stearns, Tyco, Enron, WorldCom and many others were considered pillars of our financial community and of our economy. These companies are now worthless. We must monitor our positions in a way that will maximize profits, minimize losses and yet still be time efficient. One way to accomplish this goal is to use *trailing stop loss customer orders*. This is an order set at a percentage level below the market price for our long stock positions. The trailing stop price is adjusted as the price fluctuates; it trails the price by a certain amount (usually a set percentage) that you specify. In doing so, one of the key advantages of the trailing stop-loss order is that it allows you to lock in profits rather than hold on to a stock for too long only to see your profits dissipate. While the trailing stop-loss order price will automatically rise with share prices, it will never decrease. Therefore, the stop-loss order will always be based on the stock's highest price, which is usually calculated based on closing-day prices.

Trailing Stop-Loss Example:

- You purchase shares of Company XYZ at $20 per share.
- You then set the trailing stop-loss order at 10%.

- Therefore, if the price falls to $18.00, your stock will automatically be sold.
- But as the shares of XYZ rise, so does your trailing stop-loss.
- If share price appreciates to $25, your trailing stop-loss order now sits at $22.50.
- If XYZ rises to $30, your trailing stop-loss order will be at $27.
- You can set the value to any amount you like. This could be 1%, 5%, or 50%
- **We will use a 10% trailing stop loss order in our wealth-building portfolio**

This order type will trigger automatically when share levels drop, giving you peace of mind when you're away from your computer during any significant downward action in price. <u>This order does not put a cap on profits</u>. Shares can continue to rise and you will stay invested as long as prices do not dip by 10% from its peak price. Keep in mind also that brokerages do not charge a fee for placing this order, only if it is executed.

More ways to set stop loss orders

In my view, setting trailing stop loss orders using percentiles (10% in this case) is the easiest and most practical method to avoid major losses in the stock market. However, there are other approaches that can be employed to set stop losses. Some investors will set stop loss orders when support is penetrated. In Chapter 3 (technical analysis) several charts were created depicting support via trend lines (figures 12 and 14) as well as via moving averages (figures 15 and 17). There are other technical analysis indicators that can be employed. Commonly, stop loss orders are placed <u>just below support</u> to make sure that this level is, in fact, penetrated. For example, if support is at $30, you may opt to set a stop loss order at $29.80. The reason I prefer the percentile method is that the stop loss order will change automatically whereas using trend lines, moving averages or other technical indicators will require the investor to manually change the order as required.

Disadvantage of stop loss orders

There is no guarantee you will receive the price of your stop-loss order. If the stock price drops quickly (gaps down), your order may not get filled at your predetermined stop price. Thus, you may be forced to sell at a lower price than you expected. For example, let's say XYZ reached $30 and the trailing stop was reset at $27. Now if unexpected negative news is reported and the stock price gaps down to $25, that's the price you will receive. In other words, the $27 limit order becomes a market order once that price support is broken.

When a trailing stop loss order triggers the sale of one of our stocks we turn to our watch list to select replacement equity. We divide the cash derived from the sale of the declining stock by the price per share of the new security and make our new purchase. Use the stock screener, to update the watch list if it hasn't been updated recently.

At least once a year, we should use our portfolio rebalancing strategy where we buy and sell shares in our portfolio so that each position represents approximately an equal amount of cash value.

Managing Our Stock Positions – Summary

- Enter a 10% trailing stop loss order (GTC) when originally purchasing the shares

- If the order is executed and shares sold, use the stock screener to select a replacement equity

- Divide the price-per-share of the new stock into the total amount of cash generated from the sale of the original stock to determine the number of new shares to purchase

Rebalance your portfolio at least once a year

Wealth-Building Rules in this Chapter

- Make sure your brokerage trading platform has the ability to accept trailing stop orders
- We will use a 10% trailing stop loss order on each position
- Use an online discount broker
- Open a cash account, not a margin account

Chapter 8

Stock Splits

Chapter Outline

- What is a stock split?
- Is the split an asset or a liability?
- A real life stock split example
- What is a reverse stock split?

Imagine this scenario: You check your stock portfolio and become horrified when you see one of your holdings that was trading for $50 yesterday is down to $25 today! How could a stock depreciate in value by 50% in just one day? It may be the result of a *stock split.*

What is a Stock Split?

A stock split is a change in the number of shares outstanding (in circulation). The number of shares is adjusted by the split ratio, e.g. 3 to 1. In this case, 100 shares splits to 300 shares but the price is cut by a third. Thus, the cost and current value of the investment remains the same while increasing the number of shares and decreasing the per share price. This allows retail investors to own shares in round lots (100-share increments) which they otherwise wouldn't have been able to own before the split. In other words, the stock split requires less money to buy more shares.

Is the Split an Asset or a Liability?

There are those who feel that a stock split will automatically result in a share price increase. Research seems to disprove this theory. However, a split will oftentimes occur after a significant run-up in price, after which the continuation of this trend is likely. I give credence to a stock split that occurs after such a price increase, and look at the company's chart to evaluate the momentum associated with this appreciation. When the technical indicators confirm that a stock split as legitimate (based on exceptional sound fundamentals and technicals rather than a ploy by the Board of Directors to attract attention), I consider the event as another plus in that stock's column of assets.

On the other hand, if the chart paints an ugly picture when a split is announced, it is likely that the Board of Directors for the company is desperate and looking to garner interest in a deteriorating stock. In that circumstance, the split should be viewed as a liability. Having said all that, note that it's virtually impossible that any of the stocks which pass our rigorous portfolio rules and requirements will fit into the latter category.

SHOO- A Real Life Stock Split Example

Early in 2010, Steven Madden, Ltd. (NASDAQ: SHOO) announced a 3-for-2 stock split. This means that for every 2 shares owned, 1 additional share would be distributed. The value of the shares will be worth 2/3 of the current value at the time of distribution so the *capitalization* (price x number of shares) remains the same. If your portfolio manager list showed a holding of 200 shares at $53 per share pre-split, it would show a holding of 300 shares at $35.33 post-split. Let's look at the chart (Figure 40 below) to evaluate whether this split represented an asset or a liability:

Figure 40 – SHOO - A Real Life Stock Split Example

This is a beautiful chart, uptrending with confirming indicators, describing an authentic split and an asset in the column of parameters for this equity.

Note: This stock split 3-for-2 again on 6-1-11 and was trading at $53 in September of 2013.

What is a Reverse Stock Split?

It is a reduction in the number of a corporation's outstanding shares and a corresponding increase in the value of those shares. For example, if you own 200 shares of company XYZ at $5 per share, a 1-for2 reverse stock split would result in your owning 100 shares at $10 per share. The value of your holding remains the same:

200 x $5 = $1000

100 x $10 = $1000

Reasons why reverse stock splits are done:

- It makes corporate shares look more valuable although there has been absolutely no change in real worth.
- Many institutional investors have rules against purchasing a stock whose price is below a certain minimum level, $5 perhaps. Citigroup, in 2010, fell into that category.
- Fear of being delisted from a major exchange is another possible reason. If a stock falls below a certain price, it may no longer meet the exchange requirements and face delisting or being removed from trading rights on that particular exchange.
- Reduce the number of shareholders is a *rare* but possible explanation for a reverse split. If the split results in a shareholder owning less than a minimum required number of shares, they would receive a cash payment and no shares of stock. This may be beneficial to a company seeking to be put in a different regulatory category such as an S-Corp which is required to have less than 100 shareholders.

Typically, a stock will temporarily add a "D" to the end of its ticker symbol during a reverse stock split. In most cases, the "D" will be removed after 20 trading days.

Citigroup- Real life example

In a filing with the SEC early in 2009, Citigroup, Inc. (NYSE: C) said it was considering a *reverse stock split* as part of its effort to convert *preferred shares* (take priority over common shares on earnings and assets in the event of liquidation) to common shares. Let's take a look at a chart of Citigroup as of 3-24-09 (Figure 41):

Figure 41 - Citi: A reverse stock split

You can see that Citigroup dramatically declined to a $3 per share equity. To get this to a somewhat cosmetically acceptable scenario, a 1-for-10 split would be necessary. This would elevate the share price to $30 per share. If you owned 1,000 shares at $3 before the split, you would own 100 shares at $30 after the split.

What does a reverse split signal?

In 2008, Jim Rosenfeld, an associate professor of finance at Emory University's Goizueta Business School in Atlanta, did a study involving 1600 companies that did reverse stock splits. He found that the typical stock in his study underperformed the market by 50% on a risk-adjusted basis during the three year period after the action. His conclusion:

"Reverse stock splits are a strong indicator the company is going to be a significant underperformer during the near future."

Split information can be obtained online as follows:

www.cboe.com/contractadjustments

You can also call the CBOE (Chicago Board Options Exchange) for free information:

1-888-678-4667

Chapter 9

Tax Implications

Chapter outline

- Introduction by Alan
- Personal income taxes
- Buying and selling securities
- Special circumstances
- Issues to be aware of
- Deferring income taxes
- Avoiding income taxes
- Estate and gift taxes
- Young people
- Not-so-young people
- Retirees
- Conclusion

Wealth-building portfolio rule requirements in this chapter

- Stocks should be bought and sold based on fundamental, technical and common sense principles and tax consequences should be secondary factors
- Maintain accurate records
- Consult with your tax advisor in these matters

Chapter introduction by Alan

Let me premise my remarks by stating the obvious...I am <u>*not*</u> *a tax expert. Nor do I play one on TV. However, I was quite fortunate to have Owen Sargent, an outstanding CPA and seasoned stock investor, agree to write this chapter for us.*

Thus far we have discussed how to make money investing with stocks and mutual funds. In this chapter we will address how to keep those profits. If you are investing in sheltered accounts, this information does not apply. If you are investing in non-sheltered accounts, it is important to have a basic knowledge as to how you will be taxed in your investment accounts.

You will learn in this chapter that profits from stock investments can be taxed as ordinary income or long-term capital gains. When taxed as ordinary income the tax bracket is the same as the one for your wages. It includes dividends distributed by the stock plus any short-term capital gains profit (profit from a stock sold that was held for less than one year).

Long term capital gains usually have a much lower tax consequence and applies to a profit from a stock sold that was held for at least one year and one day. Losses from stock investments can be used to offset gains and a general rule of thumb is to keep losses to a short-term status and gains to a long-term basis.

Some of the information in this chapter may not be relevant to you initially but since this is a 40-year plan, may be down the road. <u>*Use the information as a reference guide*</u>. *It is not necessary to become a tax expert but to have a general knowledge of tax-related issues can only make us all better investors.*

Three important takeaways from this chapter are:

- *Stocks should be bought and sold based on the principles discussed in previous chapters and tax consequences should be secondary factors*
- *Maintain accurate records*
- *Consult with your tax advisor in these matters*

I now turn over the tax chapter to Owen Sargent...

This chapter is NOT just about taxes. My name is Owen Sargent. I am a New York Certified Public Accountant with twenty-nine years of accounting and tax experience. I am also a New York attorney. Hopefully, my professional experiences can benefit you, and help make you the CFO of your own, and your family's, finances. You have already taken a good step in that direction when you bought this book. You also took another good step by reading this far.

This book is designed to help you be less reliant on others for investment advice. That said, there is not a single CEO in the business world who does not rely on other professionals with expertise and advice that can help them do their jobs better. It is important that you learn when you need good professional advice. I have dealt with too many clients who tried to save money by using a friend's advice, internet advice, or bad professional advice. It often winds up being much more expensive to "fix" what has already been done, if it can be fixed, than it is to pay for good professional advice in the first place. I tell my clients there is no such thing as a stupid question. Not asking the question can be very expensive. In the paragraphs that follow I hope to answer some of your unasked questions, give you some good places to do some of your own research, and to help you formulate questions for your professional advisors that are more to the point. There are two major functions of this book. The first is to help you make some money. The second is to help you keep it.

I have laid out this chapter in four parts:

- Part One: TAXES
- Part Two: YOUNG PEOPLE (I mean you, if you are between 14 and 29)
- Part Three: NOT-SO-YOUNG PEOPLE
- Part Four: RETIREES

PART ONE – TAXES

A couple of points must be made before I discuss the taxes.

First, never let the tax laws alone drive your financial planning. Tax laws are not only subject to change, they are one of the few laws that can legally be changed retroactively. The legislature cannot pass a law in August that makes something you did in the previous March illegal. They can, however, pass a tax law in August that is effective back to March, or January.

Second, refusing to make money, as a means of getting even with the government by denying them their share, is not a sound financial plan. Tax planning is important, but taxes are a societal necessity. I tell clients that my goal in life is to have a personal income tax return with a $1,000,000 income tax. That will mean that I made two, three, or even four million dollars, depending on the types of income, and the tax rates. It is much easier to win a game if you are familiar with the rules.

166

Third, my discussion of various taxes here applies to the United States of America federal taxes. Many of the readers of this book are not US citizens and, therefore, subject to entirely different taxing structures and rules. Many other readers are residents of states which have no state income taxes. Generally, state income taxes are based on your federal income, with some specific adjustments. You should discuss your state's tax issues with a competent tax preparer and/or attorney in your state. You do not need to be sufficiently knowledgeable to become a tax preparer, but you should know enough to know when you should seek professional advice, or when that advice is poor.

This chapter is being written at the end of 2012. Congress has failed to pass the necessary tax laws to allow the Internal Revenue Service to even design the 2012 income tax forms. I will not even try to discuss what is coming in 2013, because nobody has those prognostication skills. One of my favorite questions: If "pro" is the opposite of "con", is "progress" the opposite of "congress"?

Ok, let's get down to the serious tax discussion. There are two major taxes that most Americans must deal with, income taxes, and estate and gift taxes. Estate and gift taxes are actually a pair of evil twins which will be discussed simultaneously below. If you are internet inclined I strongly suggest you put **WWW.IRS.GOV** in your favorites. Please note, it is irs.**GOV**, NOT irs.**COM**. Someone has a very nice tax information website using the dot com extension. IT IS NOT THE INTERNAL REVENUE SERVICE'S WEBSITE! Each state has its own website where you may obtain state tax forms, instructions, and publications. Just be sure it is the state's official website.

I will not provide links to the IRS website because those links are subject to change from time to time. You should spend some time browsing their website, so you can find the various forms, instructions and publications discussed below.

PERSONAL INCOME TAXES

Evading taxes is illegal. Deferring taxes is desirable. Avoiding taxes is spectacular. The discussion in this section relates to activity which is not done in a retirement account. I will discuss retirement accounts later in this chapter.

Your personal income taxes are reported on **Form 1040, "U.S. individual Income Tax Return"**. Many of the numbers appearing on form 1040 come from separate schedules which must be prepared and attached to your return. Since this book is about stock and option trading you will be dealing mostly with **Schedule D, "Capital Gains and Losses"**. You will also probably need **Schedule B, "Interest and Ordinary Dividends"**, and **Schedule A, "Itemized Deductions"**. Additionally, the IRS, as of the 2011 tax year, has now made the schedule D more complicated. The transactions are no longer entered directly into schedule D. They are entered on **Form 8949, "Sales and other dispositions of Capital Assets"**. The totals appearing on forms 8949 are then transferred to schedule D. Give up yet? It gets better. You may need to prepare up to six forms 8949, depending on the nature of your transactions. Publication 17 is an excellent source of information for your personal income tax return. Another extremely important publication is 550 Investment Income and Expenses. I suggest you download these publications onto your computer (they are Adobe .pdf files) so you can print out individual pages for future reference and documentation for your income tax return.

Schedule A Itemized Deductions

Some of the items you may be able to deduct related to your investments include investment interest, such as broker margin interest (you will also need form 4952), investment expenses, such as periodic broker account fees, tax preparation fees and attorney fees. Please read the instructions for Schedule A. You should also read Publication 529 Miscellaneous Deductions.

Schedule B Interest and Ordinary Dividends

Some of the stocks, ETFs or mutual funds you own may pay you a dividend during the period you own it. This information will be reported to you on form 1099DIV. The dividend may be subject to special reduced tax rates, or it may not. Follow the instructions for schedule B and form 1040 on where to report the dividend income reported to you by the payer. <u>NOTE:</u> *The form 1099 does not have to be the government form you see on the IRS website. If you own shares of stock in a dividend reinvestment plan you may get a 1099DIV directly from that corporation or its agent. If your securities are held in a brokerage account your form 1099 will be a special report in January or February. It will have some, or all, of the same lines and descriptions as the government form, but it will probably be on 8.5" x 11" paper. Be careful. Do not to throw it out. Your tax preparer will call you many bad names, perhaps in several languages.*

Schedule D Capital Gains and Losses & Form 8949 Sales and Other Dispositions of Assets

Stock sales, and option sales beginning in 2013, are reported to you, and to the IRS, using form 1099B. As noted above, in the discussion of dividends, this form may be part of a special

169

1099 year-end report you receive from your broker. The form also may report the basis, or cost, of the security being sold. If it an option is being sold short there will be no basis information reported. If you throw this one out your tax preparer will add two zeros to his fee for preparing your returns, and still call you many bad names.

Capital gains and losses were entered directly on Schedule D in years prior to 2011. It was a simple form, at least by my standards, as a preparer. Beginning in 2011 the IRS decided to use an additional form related to the new third party information being reported to them. Form 8949 is used to list the stock, bond and option transactions individually. First, you must decide if you have a transaction where the broker has reported the cost basis of the transaction on form 1099B. Then you must decide if the transaction is short term, or long term. Hey, WAKE UP! It gets better. If you have a sale which a broker did not report you may need to prepare a form 8949 for that, too. So, conceivably, you may need SIX different forms 8949 in order to properly report your gains and losses. I am not going to get into strange transactions, such as, you sold your car for more than you paid for it (like that ever happens!), or you sold a partnership interest to another investor. If you are involved in anything like that you should be seeing a tax professional, sooner, rather than later.

Let's follow some of the transaction types you will encounter in your trading activity. Capital gains and losses result from your purchase and sale of an asset. It is important to remember, as a covered call writer (discussed in Chapter 12), that the order of the sale date and purchase date is not always the same. When you buy shares of stock you have entered into a long position. The acquisition date will be before the sale date for a long position. When you sell a covered call option, you have entered into a short position. The acquisition date will be AFTER the sale date. Do not let this confuse you when preparing the tax forms. I will restrict the discussion of short sales, and short positions, to covered call options. It is possible to sell stock short, but that is for sophisticated investors with substantial assets and substantial nerve.

The first issue is whether you have to report a transaction, or not. A short sale (selling the option when using covered call writing) is not a completed transaction which has produced a gain or a loss. You will realize a gain or a loss on the transaction only when you have "closed" the short position, by buying it back, it expires, or it is exercised. The examples below do not include any broker commissions. Be aware that all transaction costs are included in the cost basis, or subtracted from the sales proceeds, and are reported net. So, let's get on with the examples:

Buying and selling securities

Reportable transactions involve two sides, the purchase and the sale. The transaction you are probably already familiar with is "I buy 100 shares of XYZ stock. Sometime later I sell 100 shares of XYZ stock. I have a capital gain or loss, depending on the prices of each, and it is either long term, or short term, depending on how long I owned the stock. Word of advice, check the definition of "long term" from time to time. The government has changed it a few times. As of the writing of this book long term means one year, or longer. Example of reporting this gain: You bought 100 XYZ on Mar 5, 2012 for $40 per share, with a $13 broker commission. Your basis in the stock is $4,013. You sold the stock on March 1, 2013, for $50 per share, with another $13 commission. Your gross proceeds will be $4,987. This is because the proceeds are reportable net of any transaction costs on the trade. When you prepare your Schedule D you will report a short term capital gain of $1,974 ($4,987 – $4,013). It's actually pretty simple.

It gets a bit more complex when you throw in some of the special circumstances that can change your basis. You need to be aware of these so you can keep the proper records and not pay extra taxes by mistake.

Special circumstances

Example #1: Stock splits. This happens when the company decides they want to increase the shares without selling any new ones. There are a lot of reasons why they may split the stock, but they are not important to this discussion. The split may be two for one, three for one, etc. Let's take a two for one (2:1) stock split. What this means is, you bought 100 shares of ON March 5, 2012 for $40 per share, with a $13 broker commission. In October of 2012 the company split the stock 2:1. You will receive an additional 100 shares of XYZ into your account. You do not own any more of the company than you owned before. Instead of owning 100 shares out of 100 million shares you now own 200 shares out of 200 million shares. The difference is that the price will suddenly be cut in half. Before the split you owned 100 shares at say, $58 dollars per share, $5,800 worth of stock. After the split you owned 200 shares at $29 per share (still $5,800 worth of stock). Now, this is where your record keeping becomes very important! If you sell 100 shares of XYZ on March 1, 2013 your basis is NOT $4,013. It is $2,006.50. Your capital gain will be as follows: You sold 100 shares at $29. Your net proceeds will be $2,887, after $13 commission. Your basis will be $2,006.50. Your gain will be $880.50, and you will still have 100 shares with a basis of $2,006.50. If you sell the other 100 shares on April 12, 2013 for $35 per share, your proceeds will be $3,487. Your basis will be the remaining $2,006.50. Your gain will be $1,480.50, and it will be LONG term because your holding period started on March 5, 2012, NOT October 2012 when you received the additional shares.

You MUST understand this. You do NOT own 100 shares with a basis of $4,013 and 100 shares with a basis of $0! You owned 100 shares of stock in XYZ, with a basis of $4,013, bought on March 5, 2012, BEFORE the split. You owned 200 shares of stock in XYZ, bought on March 5, 2012, with a basis of $4,013 AFTER the split. The only thing that changed is the number of shares. You do NOT have a new acquisition date for the second 100 shares. Keep an eye on your brokerage report. Make sure they report it correctly. If not, call them and tell them to correct it.

Example #2: Stock dividend. This happens when the company decides to give you a dividend in shares of stock, rather than cash. First, the dividend will usually not be reportable as a dividend. Second, the math you used in the first example will get a great deal more complex. Let's say the company gives you a 5% stock dividend. Now, the 100 shares of XYZ you bought for $4,013 on March 5, 2012 has become 105 shares of XYZ you bought on March 5, 2012. If you sell 100 shares now, you will have a basis of $3,821.90 and 5 shares with a basis of $191.10. Do yourself a favor. When you sell the shares, sell the whole 105 shares. Your basis will be the original $4,013 you paid for it and you won't have a math headache later.

Example #3: Dividend reinvestment – mutual funds. This is a spectacular way of slowly building up your stock holdings.

Dividend reinvestment is very common for regular mutual funds. Most regular funds pay their dividends at the end of the year, so it is very common to get some extra shares toward the end of December. You can keep your basis on the average price method, or the specific shares method. Your broker may select a method for you. It is probably easier to use their method.

Example #4: Dividend reinvestment – common stock. Many brokers today allow you to reinvest dividends from regular stocks trades on the stock exchanges. This allows you to buy additional shares automatically, at whatever the market price is when the dividend is paid. Again, it is a great way to build up your investment portfolio. However, it creates another record keeping nightmare. You may receive 0.21345 shares for a $16 dividend on a $75 stock. If you reinvest dividends each quarter, this will happen four times each year. You will have 41 trades, each in fractions of shares, each with a $16 basis, at the end of ten years. Don't let this keep you from investing this way. It just means you need to keep proper records so you do not pay tax on the wrong capital gain when you finally sell all of the stock.

Again, you are strongly urged to double check the information being reported by your broker. The new form 1099B includes the dates of the transactions and the cost basis of the security. This information was reported to the Internal Revenue Service. If it is not correct, the first step should be to notify the broker's tax reporting department, in writing, of precisely which transactions you disagree with, and why. If the broker refuses to correct the information, you are not lost. Do the following: Report the information as the broker reported it. Then, on another line, enter transaction information which will make the totals correct. Attach a detailed schedule to your tax return explaining the adjustments. The Internal Revenue Service uses a matching program and sends out notices that they have found a difference and you are wrong. I fight these all the time. The IRS could not match a single cork to an empty wine bottle, if they were the only two objects in the room. If you can substantiate your adjustments to arrive at the correct income you will win. You may have to rub their noses in it to make them understand it, but be persistent. You are not obligated to pay an incorrect tax simply because the IRS employees don't understand what you did. <u>NOTE:</u> *Most preparers are required to e-file income tax returns. Again, do not let one tell you that the transactions must be entered individually because they cannot attach a paper schedule to an e-filed return. It is true they cannot attach a schedule, however, the IRS has bowed to taxpayer ire at the cost of keypunching each transaction. Tell your preparer to get form 8453, which can be used to mail paper documents for an e-filed return. You can find this information in the instructions for schedule D, and the instructions for form 8453.*

Some issues to be aware of

The "kiddie tax". There are special rules for minor children with unearned income. If you are trading in an account for your child, the child must file her own return. If the income exceeds a certain amount, $950 for 2011, the child's tax rate will be determined based on your tax return. This is true, even if your child is now a college student. Talk to your tax preparer if this is the case. If your child has any sales of securities she must file her own return.

The "short sale". A short sale happens when you sell before you buy. The covered call options above are a good example. You sell the option in March and buy it back in April. That is a short sale. It is unlikely that most readers of this book will be short sellers of stock, but it is possible. If you have a substantial amount of money, you can go to your broker, borrow shares of a stock and sell them short. You do this if you think the stock Is going to go down. When you buy it back at a lower price, you will make a capital gain. If you buy it back at a higher price, you will incur a loss. Just keep in mind that, for income tax reporting purposes, you report the short sale on your tax return when you buy the shares back, not when you sell the borrowed shares.

The "wash sale". This is tricky little tax issue that you need to know about. You are not allowed to take a capital loss if you bought the stock within 30 days before or after the loss sale. Example: You buy 100 shares of XYZ for $3,000. You sell them for $2,000 on December 10 for a loss of $1,000. In the meantime, you bought an additional 100 shares of XYZ for $2,100 on December 2. The government figures you have not really lost the $1,000, because you still own 100 shares of XYZ. I'm not making this up. You pay Congress to come up with this. Anyway, you have not given up the $1,000 loss forever. You just need to add it to your shares bought on December 2. You will report the $1,000 loss on your tax return, and then add it back. Then you will adjust the basis of the December 2 shares from $2,100 to $3,100. What this means is that you will essentially get your "loss" on your tax return when you finally sell the December 2 shares. Publication 550 provides a complete explanation of the tax treatment.

Deferring Income Taxes – Individual Retirement Arrangements

Most people are familiar with Individual Retirement Arrangements. Not everyone is aware you can write covered calls in an IRA account. Ask your IRA custodian. If the custodian will not allow it, consider moving the account. It is

176

probably not available in your company retirement plan, but it will not hurt to ask.

If you do sell covered calls in your IRA you can ignore the capital gains discussion above. Generally, the income earned in your regular IRA is taxed when you take distributions from the account, presumably, after you retire. If you have deducted all of the contributions into the account in previous years, all of the distributions will be taxable income in the year you take the money out. This is the definition of "tax deferred income".

You may have made contributions to your IRA which could not be deducted, because you or your spouse participated in a retirement account at work (See box 13 on your W2), and your income exceeded certain limits. If this is the case, part of your distributions in the future will not be taxed again, but the income earned on it will be. It important you keep records of your non-deductible contributions. The IRS does not do this for you, and the IRA custodian has no way of knowing whether you deducted the contribution in any particular year. You should discuss this with your tax preparer. You should also read Publication 590 Individual Retirement Arrangements.

Avoiding Income Taxes

This one is a beauty. The ROTH Individual Retirement Account. Contributions to a Roth IRA are taxed in the year you make the contribution. The income the account earns, and the original contribution, is not taxed when you take the distributions out! (Certain rules apply. Ask your tax preparer, or check Pub 590.)

NOTE: *Please, before you continue reading this book put it down and call your IRA custodian. Make sure that you have a properly updated beneficiary list. When you die your IRA*

177

account must be distributed, or transferred. Improper planning can result in a disaster for your family.

If your estate is the beneficiary the entire account will be distributed as part of the process of winding up your financial affairs. A ROTH IRA will be distributed without income tax being owed, but any future benefit that could have been derived by leaving the money in it will be lost. A regular IRA will be subject to regular income taxes on the entire distribution, and any future benefit will be lost.

If you have a beneficiary list your IRA may continue to help your beneficiaries. You may split the account among your beneficiaries as you wish. Example: You have a husband and two children. You choose to make your children the beneficiaries, at 50% each. Upon your death, the custodian will create two new inherited IRA accounts, one in each child's name. Each child must begin taking distributions each year over his or her life expectancy. The advantage is that the undistributed funds continue to earn money tax deferred. There is a special exception for your husband. He, as the beneficiary, may leave the funds in the account until he reaches 59 1/2, or he may roll the account into his own IRA that he may already have. You may read more about inherited IRAs in Publication 590.

You should update, or review the beneficiary list any time there is a change in your life. If your beneficiary list includes your ex-wife, your children and current wife will not be happy with the outcome. If you had two children when you prepared the last beneficiary list, and now you have three, your youngest child may not remember you fondly. The custodian is obligated to distribute the account according to your beneficiary list. You may not change these instructions using your will.

That pretty much covers the personal income tax subject. You need to be aware of the rules so you can better tell if your return is correctly prepared, and your preparer is not trying to make your income tax return his entire year's income.

ESTATE AND GIFT TAXES

I am not going to go into detail regarding estate taxes. If you are reading this book you are not dead, so estate taxes should not be your highest priority. Keep in mind that all of your assets, including your IRA accounts may be subject to estate taxes on Form 706. The federal estate tax begins, as of the writing of this chapter, at $5 million dollars in estate value. This means if you leave an estate worth less than $5 million on the date you die, your estate will have no tax. If you have an estate worth more than $5 million you should go see an attorney and a CPA tomorrow to do some estate tax planning. Most important: You should have a will.

Various states have estate or inheritance taxes. The difference is who the tax is levied upon, and the threshold at which the tax begins. An estate tax is levied on the estate left by the deceased individual. An inheritance tax is levied on the beneficiaries of the estate. You should have this discussion with your financial professionals sooner, rather than later.

Gift taxes are part of the estate tax scheme. The government does not want you to give your estate to your relatives before you die without getting the estate tax they will be due. A gift tax return, Form 709 is due for any year in which you give more than $13,000 (as of 2013) to any one individual, other than your spouse. Generally, there is no gift tax due, because most filers choose to use the estate exclusion ($5 million) on their gift tax returns. If you plan on giving more than $13,000 to any one individual, in one year, you should see a competent CPA before you make the gift. You should also be aware of what is specifically NOT considered a gift subject to gift tax. If you make medical payments for someone, braces, eye surgery, whatever directly to the provider of the service, the payments are not subject to gift taxes. The same rule applies for the payment of education tuition. Be careful. This does not mean you give your son a check for $25,000 to pay his tuition at Northwestern University. It means you sent the check directly to Northwestern for the tuition bill.

PART TWO: YOUNG PEOPLE

I wish I knew, when I was sixteen, what I know now. I started working as a hospital janitor, weekends and summers, during high school. It didn't pay much, and the Individual Retirement Arrangement had not yet been invented. I could easily have been retired ten years ago if I had started saving diligently way back then. Believe it, or not, if you are a young person today, you won't be for long.

I run into a number of issues with young people.

Some of you are simply ignorant when it comes to making money, saving money and investing money, but willing to learn. That's you because you are reading this book.

Some of you are simply are not interested in learning about money. That's your friend who has three different ipods, in different colors, because each one matches a different outfit. (Don't lend her any money. You won't get it back.)

Some of you have helicopter parents who do everything for you, including your income tax returns you did not know about, for that summer job you had. They give you a credit or debit card. They give you enough money so you do not need to get a job. They remove any incentive to learn to make money, save money and spend money intelligently.

Well, there is little we can do about those not interested, and those overly sheltered by their parents. But, for those of you who want to learn to be less dependent on your parents and grandparents, welcome.

Suggestion #1: Buy another book. I have given my nephews and my niece each a copy. It is another excellent book to consider. The title is *The Automatic Millionaire*, by **David Bach**. The premise is simple. Begin investing today. Invest regularly. Retire early.

Suggestion #2: Sign up for your company pension plan. Have some money invested out of each paycheck. If your employer has no pension plan, have some money deposited directly into a savings account each week. Open an IRA or Roth IRA account. Contribute each month. You may even be able to have a regular amount withdrawn from your checking account each month by the IRA custodian.

Suggestion #3: Start as early as you can. The expression "time is money" is not just some irritating phrase your boss uses to get you to hang up your cell phone and get back to work. I do not sell widgets. I am a CPA/attorney. I sell my time. The value of my time, $100/hr, $350/hr, $750/hr depends on the experience I have and my knowledge, but it is still my time that I sell, not a tangible product. There are many tables available online, or programs, that will tell you how much you can end up with if you invest $X each week or month, at Y%, for Z years. Here is a quick comparison:

If you invest $10,000 each year for 20 years, at 4% per year, you will have $309,692 at the end of 20 years. If you do not invest any additional funds for the next 20 years, the account will grow to $678,573.

If you invest $10,000 each year for 40 years, at 4% per year, you will have $988,265 at the end of 40 years.

What does this mean? Time is money. If you start when you are 20 years old, you can wind up with $678,573 when you are 60 years old, with an investment of $200,000 ($10,000 x 20 yrs). If you start when you are 40 years old, you will wind up with $309,692. The extra 20 years is worth $368,881. See? Time IS money! To quote Albert Einstein, "Compound interest is the eighth wonder of the world. He who understands it, earns it . . . he who doesn't . . . pays it."

Suggestion #4: Invest the savings carefully. You cannot replace retirement money. There are limits to how much you can contribute to various types of plans, but you cannot replace $4,000 just because you picked a lousy stock in your IRA, and it went out of business. This book is an attempt to give you some investing acumen. Not everyone is going to be comfortable selling options regularly. However, even if that describes you, you will have the knowledge that they are not for you because you learned about them first, rather than just ignoring them. Who knows, one day you may own a stock that you decide is perfect for selling a covered call to make a few extra dollars.

Just as a point of interest, a Gucci handbag is NOT an investment. Gucci stock may, or may not, be an investment, but the handbag, unless it is one of a kind, and you put in an environmentally controlled vault, is definitely not an investment. Air Jordan sneakers are not an investment. Nike stock may be. An ipod is not an investment. Apple stock may be. Do you see where I am going with this?

Suggestion #5: Don't compare your finances to someone else's. You can always find someone who is wealthier than you are. You can always find someone who is less wealthy than you are. Who cares? Your goal in life is to take care of yourself, and your loved ones. If you can also take care of some others, wonderful, but nobody is going to be more concerned with your future than you are. You can control it if you take some time to learn and some time to invest. A lottery ticket is not a retirement plan.

Suggestion #6: Learn about your tax returns. Your parents can't do it for you forever, and I do not like clients who have no idea what goes on their returns. They are the types who, two weeks after their tax returns have been filed, begin a conversation with "Oh. Is this important?" My response is generally, "No. It was important two weeks ago, but now it just means I get to charge you for amending your tax returns."

Investing is not difficult. It does not require an investment advisor. If you wear a Nylon jacket, consider investing in DuPont. If you eat Cheerios, consider investing in General Mills. If you like your Chevrolet, consider investing in General Motors. If you like your light bulbs, consider General Electric. Learn about the company and its products. Buy stock you understand. That is Warren Buffet's rule. He never bought an internet stock because he could not safely understand how they made their money. And, as we have seen, many of them didn't understand it, either. You have a serious advantage over people who are older than you are. You have more time to make up for any investing losses, and you will have losses, I promise you. You also have the time to get more money invested, and working for you, for a longer period. Start now. Retire when you are 50. Start when you are 50. Retire when you are 90. It's your choice. Be your own CEO. There is no age requirement and no interview process. Hire yourself and get started.

PART THREE: NOT-SO-YOUNG PEOPLE

Time is still money. Also, equally important, "Better late than never" comes to mind. There is a reason clichés become clichés. They are often appropriate, or true.

I know. You have responsibilities. You have a house, kids, two cars, a dog. You also have a responsibility to yourself and your retirement. There is nothing wrong with being selfish. Put your needs ahead of everyone else's. Read David Bach's The Automatic Millionaire, and then see how you feel about your next latte at Starbucks. Think about that cable premium package. Do you really need to watch Korean badminton at two in the morning? There are things you can stop wasting money on and put that money to better use, like making more money. You don't have to be putting away $30,000 per year, but $50 per week is better than nothing, and $60 per week is better than $50.

Do you realize that a car with a $290 monthly lease will get you to the same places as a car with a $490 monthly lease? What would you do with that "extra" $200 per month? The

$290 car is not as impressive as the car next to you on your way to work? Well, smile politely at the driver next to you, and quietly tell yourself you have $200 going into the bank this month that he does not. At some time in the future he will still be out here going to work, and you will be sitting in your kitchen planning your day's retirement activities.

Suggestion #1: Go sit down with a fee based financial planner. He or she may have some good suggestions that are less painful than you think. One of the things you will be required to do is to make a list of each dollar coming in and going out for a month, or two. Do that anyway. You might not even need to see a planner once you realize just how much you are spending on coffee, lunches, cable, cell phones, etc. You also need to examine the service plans you have. Get rid of the Korean badminton and knitting channels. Stop playing Words With Friends, and searching for what Kim Kardashian is doing tonight, on your cell phone.

Suggestion #2: Set an example for your children. Show them what investing can do for them if they start earlier than you did. Offer to match part of their contribution to an IRA. Talk about a return on your investment! Johnny puts $200 in an IRA and you match it? That's a 100% return on his investment before he has earned the first dime on the money.

Suggestion #3: Sit down with an attorney. Make sure your will, durable power of attorney and health care proxy is in order. DO NOT PUT THEM IN A SAFETY DEPOSIT BOX! If you are not able to access your box, the documents allowing someone else to do so are worthless, if they have to get into the box to get them.

<u>Suggestion #4</u>: Use a good tax preparer. I do not answer questions for free. However, my tax clients are able to call me and ask questions as part of my tax service to them. A client took a distribution from a retirement account simply because the company he was leaving sent him the check, in June. The following March was too late to tell him to have the funds transferred to an IRA account. He had an early distribution. It cost him taxes, penalties, and worst of all, the lost investment opportunity of those funds in a tax deferred account for the next 30 years. If you drive by my office in August you can find me here. If you drive by most H&R Block offices in August you will see a sign saying, "See you in January" and "For assistance call 1-800-TOO-LATE".

Retirement is coming, whether you are prepared for it, or not. Next time you are served that Starbucks coffee by a sixty-something year old, ask yourself, "Is she here because she WANTS to be, or because she HAS to be?" Not everyone can retire at 55 with an eight million dollar portfolio. That does not mean that it is too late for you to start saving.

PART FOUR: RETIREES

First, let's dispense with the usual "I want to leave something for my children" garbage. You left them with an existence, an education, and the best guidance you could give them. They should be out of the house now, barring some unusual situation like special needs, illness or accident. It's nice to be able to help them, and your grandchildren, but, YOU COME FIRST now.

Covered call writing is a tool for making some extra money. It is risky. It is not intended to provide you with a monthly retirement income. At this point in your life the most important thing is to not outlive your money. There are numerous devices and advices out there to help you invest your money, conserve your money, and, in some cases, relieve you of your money.

You should have a fee based financial planner, a certified public accountant and an elder care attorney. It is probably best if you get recommendations from friends. Some professionals have been known to be in cahoots with other professionals in relieving people of their money. When it comes to your money, remember Ronald Reagan's détente rule with Russia, "Trust, but verify". If you give someone the power over your money, give someone totally unrelated the ability to keep an eye the first person. Many people who wind up stealing money over long periods start out only borrowing a little. Then they can't put it back, and they need a little more. Next month they will put it back. And so on.

Annuities are useful instruments. They are essentially insurance policies. You invest a certain amount today, and the annuity company will provide you with an income stream for a fixed period of time, or until you die. There are many features, so it is wise to discuss these with your CPA. Your financial planner may be receiving a commission from the annuity, so make sure the features of the plan are what are best for you. Some are what are known as "immediate pay annuities". These begin paying you a monthly sum immediately. Others begin paying when you reach a certain age, may only pay for ten or twenty years, and may have a death benefit. Do not let the range of features keep you from considering them. They may be appropriate for your particular needs. You do not need to pick only one. You may find one immediate pay annuity, and one or two deferred annuities better fit your needs.

Social Security may be part of your retirement. Delaying collection until the latest retirement age can increase your monthly benefit. Some retirees begin collecting as early as they can, just in case they don't live long enough to collect at a later age. The monthly difference can be substantial, and it changes every year. Make sure you have someone at the local Social Security office explain it carefully to you.

Enjoy your retirement. You have earned it.

CONCLUSION

There is no magic bullet. Investing is not a Ronco rotisserie, where you set it, and forget it. You must put some time into it. You need to educate yourself on various types of investments. The rules for stocks, bonds, futures, and options are not the same. The purpose for each of them is not the same. The people who invest in them are also not the same. Your option investing should be a small part of your investment portfolio.

You will also hear people discuss things like master limited partnerships, revocable trusts, insurance trusts, mutual funds, annuities, real estate investment trusts (REITS), etc. Each of these may, or may not, be appropriate for you. As you get older you should have less invested in stocks and more liquid in savings protected by the FDIC. This is because you have less time to recover from a market downturn, and more need to use the funds you have invested for your living expenses. Learn about them. Discuss them with a trusted professional to decide what is appropriate for you. However, no matter how much you trust someone, make sure you maintain control. Investing in a publicly traded mutual fund is not giving up control. You do not have control over the investments in the fund, but you have control over owning the fund.

There is an expression regarding the television pundits you see on television, like Jim Cramer, Suze Orman, etc. They call them talking heads, because you usually only see their heads, and they often contradict each other. They may have useful information, but it may not be useful for you. You can never know too much, but you can become confused by what you know. Research your investment. Decide if it meets your investing goals. If it does, buy it. If it doesn't, don't buy it, or if you already own it, get rid of it. No stock is a lifetime hold. If it no longer meets your needs, move on. Generally big losses started out as little losses. Don't wait until you have a big loss. There is a reason why AT&T is still here, and MCI is not.

I wish you all good luck with your investing.

Wealth-building portfolio rule requirements in this chapter

- **Stocks should be bought and sold based on fundamental, technical and common sense principles and tax consequences should be secondary factors**
- **Maintain accurate records**
- **Consult with your tax advisor in these matters**

Owen Sargent is a CPA, an attorney and a seasoned stock investor. He helped me develop the Ellman Calculator and is a frequent contributor to the BCI blog forum. If you are in need of a tax advisor I recommend Owen without hesitation:

osargent@rosenblummishkin.com

Chapter 10

Other Factors that Influence Stock Performance

Chapter outline

- Earnings reports
- Company news
- Market psychology
- Key economic factors
- Globalization
- Interest rates
- Yield curves

Thus far we have discussed fundamental and technical analysis along with several common sense principles to select the best wealth-building stock candidates. On first glance, it would seem that we almost can't lose by following these system parameters. Unfortunately that is not the case. As I have stated throughout this book, there IS risk in the short run. Low risk, but risk nonetheless. There are other factors that can impact the performance of our financial soldiers. Although we don't have control over many of these circumstances, it is important to be aware of them and have a plan of action should one or more negatively impact our investment positions.

Earnings Reports

These are quarterly filings made by public companies to report their performance. They include such items as net income, earnings per share, earnings from continuing operations and net sales. These reports follow the end of each quarter. Most companies report in January, April, July and October. Certain foreign companies that trade on U.S. exchanges (American Depository Receipts or ADRs) are not required to report quarterly. Prior to these reports going public, analysts make predictions regarding the earnings and revenues about to be reported and the market reacts according to these estimates called *market consensus*. If the report beats estimates, it is called a *positive earnings surprise* and the stock can dramatically increase in price (gap up). If the stock has a negative surprise, the price can get hammered (gap down). There are sell-side and buy-side firms' estimates which are averaged together to form the *consensus estimate* for a stock. Usually, however, there is one analyst who is considered to be the leader; he or she is called the *high man* or the *ax man*. If the ax's estimates are higher than the consensus estimates, then a stock usually has to beat the ax's higher number or risk declining in price.

There is also something called a *whisper number*. This is an unofficial earnings per share (EPS) forecast that circulates among professionals on Wall Street. A report may satisfy market consensus but miss the whisper number and cause a severe price decline in the equity.

In addition to market consensus and the whisper number, many earnings reports will include *earnings guidance*. This is information that a company provides as an indication of future earnings. These guidance reports can influence analysts' stock ratings and investor decisions to buy or sell an equity.

For the long-term strategy and high-quality equities we demand for our wealth-building strategy earnings reports are less of a concern than for short-term strategies. Therefore, I discuss this topic to explain why there may be a sudden unexpected rise or decline in share price after an earnings report surprise. **There is no reason to avoid a stock when its report is due out as long as we intend to hold the equity unless it breaks our 10% trailing stop point.**

Two free websites where earnings report dates can be accessed are:

http://www.earningswhispers.com/

http://moneycentral.msn.com/investor/market/earncalendar/

Company News Other than Earnings Reports

Negative news can rear its ugly head at any time and have a devastating impact on our share price. In early 2010, MED was a high-flying stock and named the *stock of the decade* due to its incredible share appreciation. It was on my watch list and was making sensational returns for me and many other Blue Collar Investors. Then it happened! One day news came out about potential corporate fraud and the price plummeted from the mid-thirties to the teens in a matter of a few days. Our trailing stop loss order will usually keep us from incurring catastrophic losses when this occurs.

Market Psychology

Some of you may remember the dot.com explosion of the late 1990s. Internet stocks went one way only...north. You couldn't lose and returns of 25% per year just didn't seem quite enough! If you remember those good ole days you probably also remember the bursting of that bubble when the NASDAQ went from 5000 to 1300. A perfect example of greed and fear... the very same scenario we saw with the sub-prime real estate debacle that led to the recession of 2008. Once again, our trailing stop loss orders and our strict screening requirements will protect us from extreme losses.

Key Economic Indicators

These are statistics that measure current economic conditions as well as forecast trends. They are used to predict the future profit potential of public companies. These stats are made public every week, nearly every day as well. Markets react favorably or unfavorably based on their interpretation of the numbers. Here are some of the indicators that influence our equity performance:

- Inflation data
- Housing starts
- Same store sales
- Interest rates
- Bond yields
- Income statistics, hours worked etc.
- Employment statistics
- Gross Domestic Product
- Consumer Price Index (CPI)
- Producer Price Index (PPI)
- Trade deficit

- Michigan Sentiment Index
- And many more

Globalization

Our economy is no longer an entity unto itself. We are tied to the economies all over the world. The financial standing of our trading partners does matter. Currencies of other countries are important to us. A successful industrial revolution in China will bode well for corporations that may supply basic materials for their infrastructure. In my first book, *Cashing in on Covered Calls*, I alluded to the Yen Carry Trade where interest rates in Japan can impact the direction of U.S. markets. The world is becoming more complex but it is exactly this growth and expansion that will give our great corporations the opportunity to expand and grow as Blue Collar Investors all over the world take advantage of this exciting time in our history. We cannot become economists and shouldn't aspire to that goal. Even if we did, we wouldn't agree with each other just as the most highly regarded economists in the world aren't all on the same page. Let's just turn on the nightly news or listen a few minutes a day to CNBC or another financial network and get a feel for what's going in the world around us. Our wealth-building system requirements will protect us from catastrophic losses. There is no need to be a rocket scientist here. We just need to be educated, non-emotional investors and prepared to act if necessary.

Interest Rates and our Stock Market Investments

One of the economic indicators is interest rates which can have significant impact on the stock market. The importance of this subject is made crystal clear as we listen to sophisticated market investors and commentators follow every move and guidance statement made by the Fed.

The mission of the Federal Reserve is to promote economic growth and control inflation. One of the most powerful tools used in this regard is the *U.S. Federal Reserve's federal funds rate*. This is the cost that banks are charged for borrowing money from the Federal Reserve banks. It is the main way the Fed attempts to control inflation. By raising the federal funds rate, the Fed attempts to lower the supply of money because it becomes more expensive to obtain.

When the Fed Increases Interest Rates

Consumers are now paying more for credit cards and mortgage interest rates thereby decreasing the discretionary money they have to spend. This has a negative impact on a business' income and profit. Businesses themselves are affected as well, in that they tend to borrow less because the cost is more expensive. This slows down economic growth resulting in lower corporate profit.

Another negative impact that higher rates have on companies and the stock market is related to the *Discounted Cash Flow (DCF)* method of evaluating equities. Analysts determine the value of a stock by projecting its future free cash flows and then discount those figures back to the present. If a company is seen as cutting back on its growth spending, the price of the stock will decline.

When we invest in the stock market, we are incurring additional risk over treasury debt investment risk (actually considered risk-free). We do so because we anticipate a *risk premium* over and above the risk-free rate of return of (let's say) treasury bills. As the risk premium decreases, investors may

196

decide to move their capital into *substitutes*. Rising short-term interest rates tend to push up longer term bond yields making these less-risky investments more attractive and put additional pressure on stock prices. According to S&P Equity Research, twelve months after a rate hike, the S&P 500 annual returns declines to 6.2% from an overall average of 8-10% while twelve months after a rate cut, the average increases to 15.5%. This folks is why we watch the Fed and the moves and comments it makes regarding interest rates. For current data on the fed funds target rate use the following free link:

http://www.newyorkfed.org/markets/omo/dmm/fedfundsdata.cfm

When the Fed raises rates that it lends to banks, it will have a negative impact on consumers, businesses and the stock market as it attempts to control inflation.

The Yield Curve

Baseball fans know all about slow curves, knuckle curves and Uncle Charlie but a sports fanatic who invests in the market should also know about *Yield Curves*. This is a line that plots the interest rates of (most frequently) three-month, two-year, five-year and thirty-year U.S. Treasury debt (bonds and T-bills). The curve is also used to predict changes in economic growth and output. Usually, short term bonds generate lower yields to reflect the fact that they carry less risk. After all, if the economy expands, there is an expectation of increased inflation which may lead the central bank to tighten monetary policy by raising short term interest rates to slow economic growth. If interest rates are greater in the future your current investments may not look so good, hence the interest rate risk factor. Therefore, we would expect a yield curve to look like this:

197

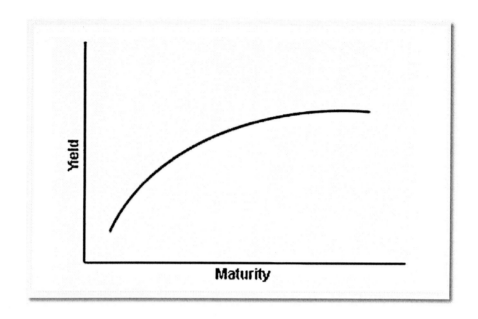

Figure 42 - Yield Curve (Normal Expectation)

There are, however, several shapes a yield curve can take. Here are some of the most important:

Normal Curve

As seen above in Figure 42, this scenario is when investors are anticipating the economy to expand at normal growth rates without significant inflation or capital availability issues. This defines a period of economic and stock market expansion and good news for investors and economists. The yield curve slopes *gently* upward as bond (longer term treasuries) investors demand more of a return to counterbalance interest rate risk in the future.

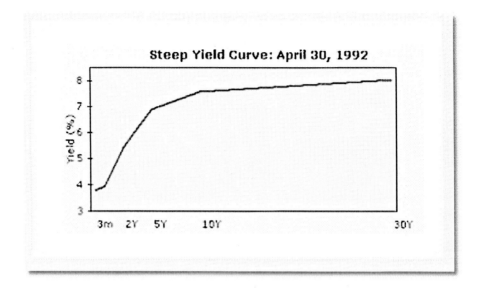

Figure 43 - Steep Yield Curve- 1992

This results when we have a greater-than-normal gap between the shorter and longer term treasuries as we see here in April of 1992. This marks the beginning of an economic expansion shortly after a recession. By 1993, the GDP was expanding by 3% per year and by the following year short-term interest rates had increased by 2 percentage points. That's why investors were demanding greater long-term returns. Those investors who used this curve to increase their stock holdings were rewarded with a 20% return over the next two years (Russell 3000).

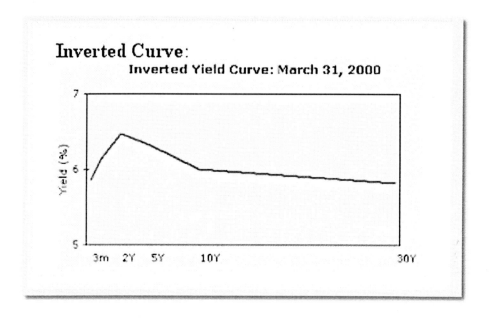

Figure 44 - Inverted Yield Curve (2000)

An inverted curve occurs when long-term yields fall below shorter-term yields. Long- term investors are betting that the economy will decline in the future. An inverted yield curve has predicted a worsening economy in the future 5 out of 6 times since 1970. The N.Y. Federal Reserve regards this yield shape to be predictive of recessions two to six quarters ahead. Stock investors should take this situation seriously. Inverted curves are rare, but when they do occur, are almost always followed by economic slowdown, or even recession.

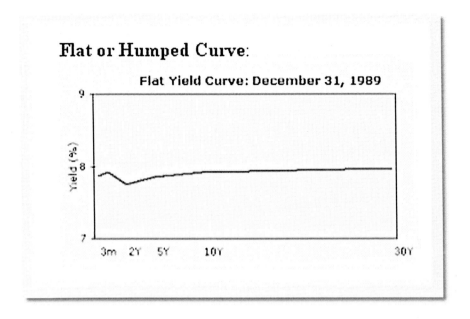

Flat or Humped Curve:

Figure 45 - Flat or Humped Yield Curve-2008-09

In the case of a flat curve, all maturities have similar yields. For humped curves, short and long-term maturities are the same while intermediate maturities are higher. It is important to note that for a yield curve to become inverted, it must pass through this phase first. Now, not all flat or humped curves become inverted but most are predictive of economic slowdown and lower interest rates. Like inverted curves, a flat or humped curve is a red flag for stock investors.

Here is a free website to access the current yield curve:

http://www.bloomberg.com/markets/rates/index.html

Conclusion

There are a myriad of factors that may impact our stock positions and the overall value of our wealth-building portfolios. Understanding these factors is critical to becoming informed, successful investors. **By adhering to our core wealth-building principles, the opportunities for achieving our goals far exceed those who are uninformed.**

Chapter 11

Related Topics of Interest

Chapter Outline

- Illegal scams
- S&P futures and fair value
- CBOE Volatility Index- VIX
- After hours trading

Illegal Scams

Pump and Dump

I'll bet that each and every one of you has received an email that went something like this:

IMAGINE IF YOU HAD THE CHANCE TO BUY A WAL-MART FRANCHISE IN MEXICO RIGHT WHEN IT FIRST OPENED ITS DOORS THERE AND ALL YOU NEEDED WAS A SMALL STAKE TO GET IN.

Hurry, we see this stock starting to make the turn NOW. Big watch in effect for November 15th, 2009!!!!

What a great guy this must be to send me this information and to be so concerned about my financial well-being! The truth is that you are now being presented with the bait for a pump and dump *scam*.

A *pump and dump scam* is a form of microcap (companies with small capitalizations, between $50 million and $300 million) stock fraud, which attempts to artificially **pump up** the price of equity through false, misleading or exaggerated statements. The perpetrators of this scheme, who already have a position in the stock, **dump** their securities after the hype has caused a spike in the share price. The victims of these scams usually lose a considerable portion of their investment as the price subsequently plummets. Perhaps that fellow who sent the email wasn't such a nice guy after all!

In the past, pump and dump schemes were initiated through cold calling, however the internet has opened the doors for a new breed of fraudsters. Scammers now have a cheaper, easier and faster way to reach an enormous number of unsuspecting victims. We must not let greed and temptation overtake our sense of reality. We know how to locate great investment opportunities through fundamental and technical analysis. This is a far superior approach than listening to "some guy" who we never met.

Oftentimes pump and dump scams take on multi-level, more sophisticated formats. For example, there may be e-mail and telemarketing campaigns supported by newsletters highlighting a particular company as a "hot stock pick." Chat rooms may be flooded with pleas for investors to "hurry-up and buy this red-hot stock." Give me a _____ break (feel free to fill in the blank).

Why Micro Caps?

Pump and dump scams work best with small, thinly traded companies called "penny stocks." Penny stocks are equities that trade at low price (under $5 per share) and have small market capitalization (# of outstanding shares x share price). They usually trade over the counter through pink sheets and bulletin boards. They are considered extremely risky due to their lack of liquidity, large bid-ask spreads, and limited analyst following and disclosure. There is also a class of even smaller companies called *nano-caps,* which typically have market capitalization under $50 million. If you follow the wealth-building rules and requirements set forth in this book, it will be virtually impossible for you to fall victim to a pump and dump scam.

Painting the Tape

Painting the tape is an illegal action whereby fraudsters buy and sell securities amongst themselves to create an artificial appearance of trading activity, which is then reported on the ticker tape (reported publically). This "trading activity" (which is really smoke and mirrors) may catch the attention of unsuspecting investors, who perceive the high volume activity as institutional interest and consequently take positions in the stock, which raises the stock's price. The fraudsters then sell their own stock as the artificially inflated stock prices peak, and retail investors take the hit. The SEC is all over this one as well.

Illegal Scams - Conclusion

Forget about that Wal-Mart in Mexico, and let's stick to our system of fundamental and technical analysis to locate our investment candidates. This will protect our hard-earned money and force those scammers to get real jobs just like the rest of us.

S&P Futures and Fair Value

You turn on CNBC early one morning:

The S&P Futures are UP 5 points.....GREAT!!!!!!!!!!

Fair Value is + 10.......what's that mean?

The market is expected to open DOWN.......ughhhh......why?

To understand how this works, we need to first understand the relationship between a financial index (in this case the S&P 500) and its index futures:

Financial Index vs. Index Futures

The S&P 500 Index - This is an index of 500 stocks chosen for market size (large cap), liquidity and industry grouping. It is one of the most commonly used benchmarks used to reflect the overall U.S. stock market.

Index Futures - These are contracts specifying a future date of delivery of the underlying instrument (the S&P 500 index). Buying or selling a futures contract represents a bet on the future direction of how the index will behave over time. Its value fluctuates according to what traders are willing to pay for it. The *futures* for the S&P 500 and the actual S&P 500 are NOT the same thing. Since stocks historically rise in value (although you couldn't tell that from the debacle of 2008!), the futures lead and are generally higher than the actual index. These contracts expire quarterly (March, June, September and December) and are usually quoted in reference to the *next* expiring futures contract.

Fair Value - This is the relationship between the futures contract or *expected value* in the future and the *present value* or current *cash value* of the index. When calculating fair value, investment banks and brokerages must also factor in *borrowing costs* to own all the stocks in the index as well as the *dividends* that are NOT received by those who own the futures contracts. For example, if the fair value is calculated at +5, the futures contract needs to be 5 points above the cash index's (S&P 500) close the previous day to be at its fair value relationship to cash. If it is, then the present value and future value are equal and traders are expecting no change in the market value of the index. However, if before the market opens, the futures are trading above the fair value of +5, stocks are likely to open higher. Fair value does not change during the course of a day, only day-today.

Hypothetical Example

- The S&P 500 *Index* closes Monday at 1000 (4PM, EST)

- S&P *futures* closed at 1005 (9:15 AM)

- *Fair value* for the futures, when factoring in borrowing costs and lost dividends, was calculated to be 1010 or + 5.

- On Tuesday morning when futures ended their overnight trading (9:15 AM, EST), the price was at 1015 or 5 points higher than their fair value relationship to cash value of the S&P 500 index. This indicates a higher market open. Had the futures ended their overnight trading at 1005 that would have been 5 points lower than fair value indicating a lower opening.

Program Trading

When the spread is greater or lesser than fair value, institutional computerized programs kick in to buy or sell stocks. If the spread or premium of futures as it relates to cash (S&P 500 Index) is greater than fair value, the market will see a higher open. If the spread is lower than fair value, the market will open down. These programs are automatic and will quickly diminish the difference between actual spread and fair value.

This will create a temporary volatility in the market which will quickly calm down.

Figure 46 below shows what a typical fair value/futures screen looks like:

Figure 46 - Screen comparing fair value to futures value

S&P Futures and Fair Value - Conclusion

Understanding the concept of fair value as it relates to S&P futures and the index itself will not influence stock selection. What it will do for us is to explain the driving forces behind a market open and differentiate *program trading* from *panic selling* and *buying sprees* which are driven by business and/or market conditions. It will also give some meaning to that screen we have been staring at in the morning for all these years.

The CBOE's Volatility Index (VIX)

In all my books and seminars I discuss determining market tone before making any investment decisions. One of the main factors I utilize in this determination is the VIX.

The VIX is the ticker symbol for the Chicago Board Options Exchange (CBOE) Volatility Index, which is a measure of the implied or expected volatility of S&P 500 options over the next 30 days. This implied volatility is reflected in the premiums paid for the options. It is constructed using the implied volatilities of a wide range of S&P 500 index options. This volatility is meant to be forward looking and is calculated from both calls and puts. The VIX is a widely used measure of market risk and is often referred to as the "investor fear gauge".

There are three variations of volatility indexes: the VIX tracks the S&P 500, the VXN tracks the Nasdaq 100 and the VXD tracks the Dow Jones Industrial Average.

The VIX is a useful indicator for short-term investors, including 1-month covered call writers (discussed in the next chapter). Generally speaking, as market volatility increases, the general market pricing of securities in general will diminish and vice-versa. The VIX is said to have an inverse relationship with the S&P 500. If we see a declining VIX or one that is remaining stable at a low level (below 30) along with an appreciating S&P 500, we have a favorable environment for stock investing.

Figure 47 shows the inverse relationship between the VIX and the S&P 500 over a 3- month time frame:

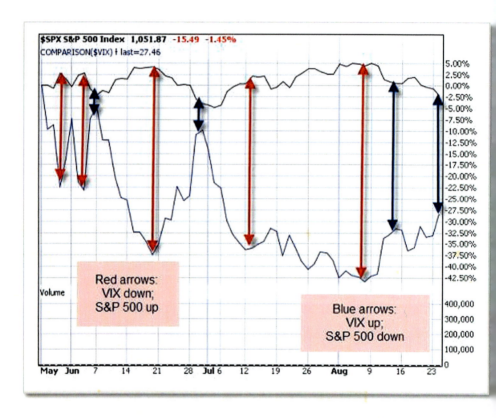

Figure 47 - The VIX vs the S&P 500

The red arrows highlight areas when the VIX was declining and the S&P 500 was appreciating and the blue arrows show just the opposite. This relationship is not 100% accurate but it does add information that will help guide us in our investment decisions especially as they relate to shorter-term strategies. Like all other technical tools the VIX should be used in conjunction with other fundamental, technical and common sense indicators

After Hours Trading

It's 4 PM EST and the bell rings on the New York Stock Exchange marking the end of the trading day. As we watch CNBC, Bloomberg or Fox Business News we see the tickers till scrolling at the bottom of our TV screens! What's up with that? The New York Stock Exchange and the Nasdaq Stock Market—the highest volume market centers in the U.S. today—have traditionally been open for business from 9:30 a.m. to 4:00 p.m. EST. Although trading outside that window—or "after-hours" trading—has occurred for some time, it used to be limited mostly to high net worth investors and institutional investors.

But that changed by the end of the last century. Some smaller exchanges now offer extended hours. And, with the rise of Electronic Communications Networks, or ECNs, everyday Blue Collar Investors can gain access to the after-hours markets. Before you decide to trade after-hours, you need to educate yourself about the differences between regular and extended trading hours, especially the risks. While after-hours trading presents investing opportunities, there are also the following risks for those who want to participate (Information extracted directly from the Securities and Exchange website):

"Inability to See or Act Upon Quotes: Some firms only allow investors to view quotes from the one trading system the firm uses for after-hours trading. Check with your broker to see whether your firm's system will permit you to access other quotes on other ECNs. But remember that just because you can get quotes on another ECN does not necessary mean you will be able to trade based on those quotes. You need to ask your firm if it will route your order for execution to the other ECN. If you are limited to the quotes within one

system, you may not be able to complete a trade, even with a willing investor, at a different trading system.

Lack of Liquidity: Liquidity refers to your ability to convert stock into cash. That ability depends on the existence of buyers and sellers and how easy it is to complete a trade. During regular trading hours, buyers and sellers of most stocks can trade readily with one another. During after-hours, there may be less trading volume for some stocks, making it more difficult to execute some of your trades. Some stocks may not trade at all during extended hours.

Larger Quote Spreads: Less trading activity could also mean wider spreads between the bid and ask prices. As a result, you may find it more difficult to get your order executed or to get as favorable a price as you could have during regular market hours.

Price Volatility: For stocks with limited trading activity, you may find greater price fluctuations than you would have seen during regular trading hours. News stories announced after-hours may have greater impacts on stock prices.

Uncertain Prices: The prices of some stocks traded during the after-hours session may not reflect the prices of those stocks during regular hours, either at the end of the regular trading session or upon the opening of regular trading the next business day.

Bias Toward Limit Orders: Many electronic trading systems currently accept only limit orders, where you must enter a price at which you would like your order executed. A limit order ensures you will not pay more than the price you entered or sell for less. If the market moves away from your price, your order will not be executed. Check with your broker to see whether orders not executed during the after-hours trading session will be cancelled or whether they will be automatically entered when regular trading hours begin. Similarly, find out if an order you placed during regular hours will carry over to after-hours trading.

Competition with Professional Traders: Many of the after-hours traders are professionals with large institutions, such as mutual funds, who may have access to more information than individual investors.

Computer Delays: As with online trading, you may encounter during after-hours delays or failures in getting your order executed, including orders to cancel or change your trades. For some after-hours trades, your order will be routed from your brokerage firm to an electronic trading system. If a computer problem exists at your firm, this may prevent or delay your order from reaching the system. If you encounter significant delays, you should call your broker to determine the extent of the problem and what you can to get your order executed"

Chapter 12

Covered Call Writing: Using Stock Options to Enhance Returns

Chapter outline

- Real estate example
- Stock market example
- Covered call writing definitions
- Components of an options contract
- Portfolio overwriting
- Summary of covered call writing in our wealth-building portfolio

Important note about this chapter: It is not necessary to study and master the information in this chapter. I decided to include a chapter on covered call writing as a brief introduction to a stock and option strategy that I have written about in my first three books. Concentrate on the first 11 chapters of this book. Once you have launched your wealth-building portfolio and your journey to financial independence take a look at this chapter and see if it piques your interest. This information represents an opportunity to potentially bring your profits to even higher levels.

Thus far in our wealth-building strategy we have created two income streams:

- Share appreciation

- Dividend capture and re-investment

As you get more confident with your investing acumen (and you will) there is a way to create a third income stream through the use of stock options using a strategy called *covered call writing*. This strategy is the main focus of the first three books I authored. **It is NOT essential that you use this strategy in your wealth-building portfolio but for those looking to enhance profits to the highest possible levels and willing to put in a little extra time and effort read on.**

Before we get into the specifics of covered call writing, it will be helpful to give two preview examples. Having the general concept in mind will facilitate learning the particulars much less cumbersome. In general, the concept of <u>selling</u> options works like this: You purchase an asset like a house or a stock and then sell some unknown person (trading is done online) the right, but not the obligation to purchase that asset from you at a specific price (that YOU determine), by a specific date (that YOU determine). In return for undertaking this obligation, you are paid a premium (that the MARKET determines). The cash is generated into your account instantly and available for immediate investment or whatever you chose to do with it. In our wealth-building portfolio, we would use this cash to purchase additional shares. First I will demonstrate with a real estate example and then bring it into the world of the stock market.

Real Estate Example

You do your due-diligence and purchase a property for $100k. You feel comfortable that the property will increase in value and would have no problem owning the property for the long term. However, if you were offered $120k for this property at any time over the next six months, you would accept it for a quick $20k profit. Now along comes investor OB (the option buyer). He loves your property and feels that it could appreciate in value up to $150k during the next six months. However, Mr. OB has many other investments and doesn't want to risk $120k at this time but he sure would like to *control* this property. He offers you $10k for the right, *but not the obligation*, to purchase your property for $120k at any time over the next six months. This 10k option premium is yours to keep whether OB exercises the option and buys your property or not (in many real estate deals the premium IS applied to the purchase price but this is NOT how it works in the stock market so for this example, you keep the premium under all circumstances). After the six month period, there are two possible outcomes:

Scenario I:

The option is not exercised and you keep both the premium and the property. This would occur when the value of the property never surpasses the agreed upon $120k sales price. After all, why would OB buy your property for $120 when he could buy a similar property for less money? In this case, you garner a $10k profit on an investment of $100k which is a 10%, 6-month return or 20% annualized. You are now free to sell another option on the same property.

Scenario II:

The option is exercised and the property is sold for $120k as per your obligation. Let's say that OB was correct and the value of the property appreciated to $150k. He can buy the property from you at $120k and sell it at market for $150k, making a nice profit. We, however, are the option sellers, so let's see how we made out in this second possible outcome. We have the $10k option premium PLUS an additional $20k profit on the sale of the property for a total profit of $30k. On an investment of $100k, that represents a six month profit of 30% or 60% annualized.

From the description of the two possible outcomes, it almost looks like you can't lose. Unfortunately and realistically, that's not the case. If the value of the property declines in value by more than the option premium received, you start to lose money. The cost of the asset minus the option premium received is known as the *breakeven*. In this example, if the property value depreciates under $90K, you will be in a losing situation. However, you will have lost less money than the investor who purchased a similar property and didn't sell an option. **The risk is in the underlying asset, not in the sale of the option.**

Stock Market Example

In this case, the underlying asset is stock instead of property. You purchase 100 shares of company XYZ at $48 per share. Your investment or cost basis is therefore $4800. Once again, you now sell the option. You are selling the right, but not the obligation, for some unknown person (Mr. OB) to buy your shares for (in this hypothetical) $50 per share at any time over the next (in this hypothetical) *one* month. A fair premium for this would be $1.50 per share or $150 for the 100 shares. This cash is generated into your account immediately and yours to keep whether the option is exercised or not. Let's examine the two possible outcomes.

Scenario I:

The stock value does not supersede the $50 agreed upon sales price and the shares are not sold. You have profited $150 on a $4800 investment or a 3.1%, 1-month return, 38% annualized. You are now eligible to sell another option on those same shares.

Scenario II:

The stock value does surpass the $50 agreed upon sales price and the option is exercised as the stock is sold for $50 per share. You have now generated $150 from the option sale plus $200 profit from the sale of the stock for a total of $350. This represents a 7.3%, 1-month return, or 87% annualized.

Once again, bear in mind that there is some risk in this strategy. The risk is in the stock. If the stock depreciates in value by more than the $1.50 per share generated from the option sale, you will start to lose money. Your loss will be less than an investor who bought the stock and didn't sell the corresponding option. With this general concept in mind, let's move on to the basics of options and covered call options in particular.

Covered Call Writing Definitions

It is essential to understand all the terminology related to covered call writing in order to be successful. In other words, we must "talk the talk." New investors should read through these terms now and refer back to them as needed until they become second nature to you.

General Terms

Call option - the right, but not the obligation of the option holder (buyer), to BUY 100 shares of stock at a fixed price by a specified date.

Covered call writing - Implicit in the term covered call writing is the fact that we are selling call options. They are covered because we first own the underlying equities prior to selling the option. We are purchasing stock and selling the corresponding options on a share-for-share basis. One option contract = 100 shares; 5 contracts = 500 shares and so on.

Opening and Closing a Position- When we sell (write) a call option, it is referred to as opening a position. Since we sold the contract we are said to be opening a short position. The holder (buyer) has opened a long position. We, as the option seller, can close our position by purchasing the same contract. That will cancel the original sale and now you will own the stock long (simply stock ownership). Buying back options contracts is the basis for our covered call writing exit strategies.

Option - the right, but not the obligation, to buy or sell 100 shares of stock at a fixed price (called the *strike price*) by a specified date (called the *expiration date*). It is the right to execute a stock transaction.

Option chain - A way of quoting option prices through a list of all the options for a given security. For each underlying security, the option chain tells investors the various strike prices,

220

expiration dates, and whether they are calls or puts. All brokerages provide option chain quotes.

The Option Contract - The option sets the terms of a contract about a possible future transaction involving the underlying stock. Since the option value is directly related or derived from that security, options are said to be derivatives. When the holder of the option makes use of the right granted by the option, the contract is said to be exercised. It is important to remember that until that option is exercised (it may never be exercised) the option writer retains all rights conferred by stock ownership. For example, if a dividend is distributed prior to the security changing hands, the option seller will enjoy those profits.

Put option- the right, but not the obligation of the option holder, to SELL 100 shares of stock at a fixed price by a specified date.

Option Strike price as it relates to the Stock Price

At-the-money (A-T-M) - the value of the underlying stock is identical to the strike price of the option. An example is when you sell the $50 call option on a stock currently trading at $50. Closely related to A-T-M strikes are *near-the-money strikes* where the stock value is close to but not exactly the same as the market value of the stock. For example, if the stock is trading at $50.10, the $50 call option is said to be near-the-money.

In-the-money (I-T-M) - the value of the stock is higher than the strike price of the option. An example is when you sell a $50 call option on a stock trading at $52.

Out-of-the-money (O-T-M) - the value of the stock is lower than the strike price of the option. An example is when you sell a $50 call option on a stock trading at $48 per share as demonstrated in our preview example.

Option Value as it relates to Strike Price

Intrinsic value- This is the dollar amount that the option premium is in-the-money. Only I-T-M strikes have intrinsic value as a component of the option premium

Time value – The option premium above any intrinsic value.

Here is an example of these last two definitions:

- *Purchase a stock for $56 per share*
- *Sell the $50 call option for $8*
- *The option strike price is $6 in-the-money ($56 - $50). This is the intrinsic value. The remaining premium value is therefore time value of $2 ($8 - $6 = $2). The critical equation to remember is:*
- *Option Premium = Intrinsic Value + Time Value*

Components of an Options Contract

In February of 2010, the options symbology changed. The previous option ticker symbols consisted of the root symbol of the underlying security ("QAA" below), then a letter that signified both the expiration date and whether we are dealing with a call or put option ("E" below) and then a letter that described the strike price ("D" below):

The *former* ticker symbol looked like this: QAA-ED. Books on options published prior to 2010 will show this option symbology.

The *new* or *current* Symbols now look like this (figure 48):

FIGURE 48 – New Option Symbology

- AAPL is the ticker symbol of the stock
- 05/22/2010 is the expiration date, the third Friday of April
- "20.00" is the strike price
- "C" represents a call option

Portfolio Overwriting

Selling Covered Calls on Stocks You Want to Keep

Most covered call writers purchase a stock specifically for the purpose of selling the corresponding call option. The investment time frame is generally short-term. In many cases share assignment is permitted by the seller and even if early assignment occurs, our investment would still have been a successful one. In other words, losing (selling) the stock is no problem and really just part of the strategy.

There are other investors who sell call options in a different manner, called *portfolio overwriting*. **This is how covered call writing relates to our wealth-building strategy to retire a millionaire at a young age.** In this instance, a call option is sold on a stock already part of our existing portfolio. That option is selected in a manner where the option is NOT expected to be exercised. Remember that **you need to own 100 shares for every options contract sold**.

Why a Portfolio Overwriter Does Not Want His Shares Assigned:

This is basically a tax issue. The holding period for short-term versus long-term capital gains is one year. If the stock has been held for less than that time frame, the writer would prefer to retain the equity for a longer time frame assuming there was share appreciation. In addition, if the shares have appreciated substantially from the cost basis, selling in any time frame may not be in the investor's best interest. **This does not apply to sheltered accounts.** *Another reason portfolio overwriters may not want their shares sold is to capture dividends for dividend-bearing stocks in their portfolios.*

Another important tax issue:

If the underlying stock has not accumulated the full 1-year holding period for long-term capital gains, covered call writing may suspend or eliminate the current accumulated holding period. It is advisable to consult with your tax advisor on this matter.

Advantages of portfolio overwriting

- Achieve higher returns in declining, neutral and slightly bullish markets
- Beat the returns of long-term holders of equities
- Increase portfolio downside protection, thereby minimizing risk
- Generate a monthly cash flow
- Use option profits to compound your money

Strike selection for portfolio overwriting

Since our goals are to generate a monthly cash flow and NOT have our shares assigned, common sense dictates that we sell out-of-the-money strikes (higher than the current market value of the stock). Remember, we don't want our option strike price ending up in-the-money. Our mindset needs to be slightly different when selling these out-of-the-money strikes in that a 2-4%, 1-month return (I use for short-term covered call writing) is too lofty a goal. I would set it more at 1-1 1/2% per month, ensuring that the implied volatility (IV) of the option is not too high. A high IV means that the market is anticipating a large price movement and that increases the possibility of the option ending up in-the-money. So settle for a lower premium and therefore less chance of assignment. As a guideline, I like to see the *share price at least 5% lower than the strike sold*. As an example, if I sold a $50 strike, I would want that equity to be currently trading at $47.50 or less, with the option premium generating 1% to 2%. In Figure 49 below is the options chain for GMCR, one of the stocks in our sample portfolio:

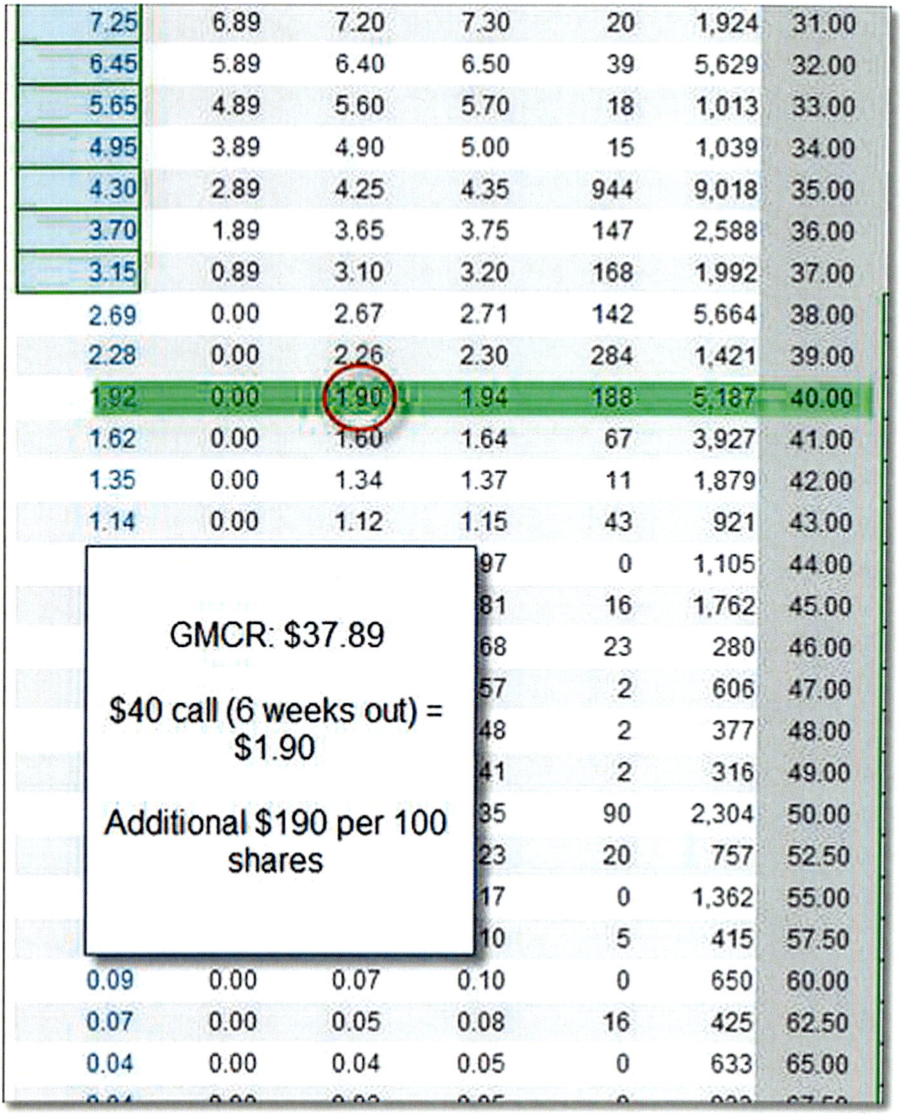

7.25	6.89	7.20	7.30	20	1,924	31.00
6.45	5.89	6.40	6.50	39	5,629	32.00
5.65	4.89	5.60	5.70	18	1,013	33.00
4.95	3.89	4.90	5.00	15	1,039	34.00
4.30	2.89	4.25	4.35	944	9,018	35.00
3.70	1.89	3.65	3.75	147	2,588	36.00
3.15	0.89	3.10	3.20	168	1,992	37.00
2.69	0.00	2.67	2.71	142	5,664	38.00
2.28	0.00	2.26	2.30	284	1,421	39.00
1.92	0.00	1.90	1.94	188	5,187	40.00
1.62	0.00	1.60	1.64	67	3,927	41.00
1.35	0.00	1.34	1.37	11	1,879	42.00
1.14	0.00	1.12	1.15	43	921	43.00
			97	0	1,105	44.00
			81	16	1,762	45.00
			68	23	280	46.00
			57	2	606	47.00
			48	2	377	48.00
			41	2	316	49.00
			35	90	2,304	50.00
			23	20	757	52.50
			17	0	1,362	55.00
			10	5	415	57.50
0.09	0.00	0.07	0.10	0	650	60.00
0.07	0.00	0.05	0.08	16	425	62.50
0.04	0.00	0.04	0.05	0	633	65.00

GMCR: $37.89

$40 call (6 weeks out) = $1.90

Additional $190 per 100 shares

Figure 49 - A typical options chain

If the share price remains below $40 by expiration Friday (the third Friday of the month) no action is needed on your part and you're free to sell another option the next month. If the share price is above the strike price ($40) you can roll the option (buy it back and sell the next month option). *If you need cash to buy back the options and don't have it in your account, you can sell enough shares to buy back the options and retain a majority of the original shares. In keeping with our cash allocation and portfolio rebalancing requirements we would tend to sell shares that have appreciated the most and have a dominant position in our portfolio.*

What if early assignment occurs?

This will not occur often but it can eventually happen. If there is a tax issue, purchase an amount of shares equal to the obligation to deliver and notify your broker that these newly acquired shares should be identified as the shares delivered to meet the option obligation. *Check with your broker, before the fact, as to the best way to manage such scenarios.*

Conclusion

Portfolio overwriting provides many of the advantages of the buy-write strategy but because of tax implications and possibly dividend capture issues income goals and strike management differ and need to be fully understood before taking action.

Summary of covered call writing in our wealth-building portfolio

- Sell call options that are at least 5% out-of-the-money

- Target 1-month returns of 1-1/2%

- If the strike price is not reached, sell another option the next month

- If the stock price is greater than the strike price as 4PM EST is approached on expiration Friday, roll the option to the next month (example: buy back January $40 call and sell February $40 or $45 call)

- If your shares are sold early (very rare) and there are tax consequences, purchase new shares and identify the new shares as the ones sold (check with your broker)

- If you need cash to roll your options, sell a few shares and retain the majority of your shares

It is beyond the scope of this book to present all the detailed information needed to master the strategy of covered call writing. For more detailed information on covered call writing, visit my web site:

www.thebluecollarinvestor.com

Appendix I

Strategy Outline

- Raise $1000.00 to open a brokerage account

- Purchase a broad market index mutual fund such as SWTXS or SWPPX

- On a monthly basis, invest (dollar-cost-average) one twelfth of 10% of your gross annual income to purchase additional shares of the mutual fund (minimum of $100.00 per purchase)

- 5-months prior to reaching $25,000, start dollar-cost-averaging $1000.00 per month per stock into 5 different equities using 10% trailing stops with each purchase

- All the while, continue investing one twelfth of 10% of your gross annual income into your mutual fund account on a monthly basis

- When your mutual fund account builds back up to $5000.00 + (with enough extra cash to keep the account open) invest an additional $1000.00 into each of your 5 equities again using trailing stops with each stock purchase

- Increase the number of different stocks as your portfolio value grows:

  $100k: up to 10 stocks

  $200k: up to 15 stocks

  $300k and up: up to 20 stocks

- If the trailing stop is filled and your shares sold, use the screener or your watch list to select a replacement stock and make a new purchase and add in the trailing stop order

- Rebalance your portfolio at least once a year

Appendix II

Online Discount Brokers

Online Discount Brokerages- what to look for

In the early 1990s when I started investing in the stock market, trade commissions were a major factor impacting our bottom line results. Commissions of $50, $100 and even $200 per trade were common debits seen on our statements. The internet has nurtured a change in trading costs through an explosion of online discount brokers. We can now trade at greatly reduced commissions but in return receive no personalized advice. This is the perfect scenario for Blue Collar Investors who have educated themselves to the point where we need no assistance as we do our own due-diligence. Furthermore, selling predominantly 1-month covered calls requires many trade executions and the need for commissions to be non-events is essential to maximizing our returns. When deciding on which online discount broker to use, I would factor in the following:

- Low trade commissions
- Efficient trade executions
- Watch out for hidden fees and minimum requirements
- Prompt and courteous phone service should be available if a problem arises
- Depending on your volume, you may be able to get access to their "advanced platforms."

I started using USAA Brokerage Services in the early 1990s as I was an officer in the military and at the time that allowed me to take advantage of this service. Since then, anyone can use this service and I do highly recommend it. Over the years, fellow Blue Collar Investors have recommended other online discount brokers to me and other members of the BCI community. Although I have no first hand knowledge of these other brokerages, I will include them on the following list and you can do your due-diligence checking them (and others) to see which meet your needs.

USAA: www.usaa.com

$5.95 PER TRADE + $0.75 PER OPTION CONTRACT

ZECCO: www.zecco.com

10 free stock trades every month so long as you maintain a $25,000 minimum balance or make at least 25 trades each month. However, even if an account is unable to satisfy the requirements to get the free trades, the regular Zecco commission rate is only $4.50 per trade

TRADE KING: www.tradeking.com

$4.95 per trade. Whether online or broker assisted, trades via the popular brokerage firm at a mere $4.95 per equity trade for both market and limit transactions. With TradeKing, there are no minimum balance requirements and no account maintenance fees.

SCOTTRADE: www.scottrade.com

$7.00 per online trade with no account maintenance or inactivity fees, and low balance requirements. While phone and broker assisted trades do cost more, they can be easily avoided by simply sticking with online trades exclusively.

TRADEMONSTER: www.trademonster.com

$7.50 per trade up to 5,000 shares, and $0.50 per options contract

E*TRADE: www.etrade.com

$9.99 per equity trade for those who make at least 30 trades a month or maintain $50,000 in account assets, and charging the standard rate of $12.99 per trade otherwise.

CHARLES SCHWAB: www.schwab.com

On-line trades - $8.95 per equity trade plus $0.75/options contract. You can negotiate lower prices based on your account and trade volume.

Other sites to consider:

www.thinkorswim.com

www.tdameritrade.com

www.optionsxpress.com

http://www.interactivebrokers.com/ibg/main.php

Link for updates on several brokerages:

www.brokerage.com/stocktrading.html

It is important to do your own research assuring that you will be receiving the lowest possible commissions while still receiving outstanding online service.

For establishing accounts outside the US, look into the following:

- Charles Schwab

- Zecco

- TradeMonster

- Options Express

- Interactive Brokers

Long-Term Chart of S&P 500

Figure 50 - (1972 – 2012 in the yellow field)

Appendix IV

Stock Selection Requirements

Descriptive Requirements

- Share price of $15 or higher
- Market-cap of $2 billion or greater
- Average daily trading volume of 500,000 shares per day or higher

Fundamental Requirements

- We will require our stocks to have PEG ratios of "2" or less
- We will require our equities to have ROEs of 15% or higher
- We will require our shares to have achieved a positive sales growth rate during the past 5 years
- We will require our stocks to have positive EPS growth during the past 5 years
- We will require our stocks to have projected EPS growth of 10% or greater over the next 5 years
- We will require our securities to have P/B Ratios of "4" or less

Technical Requirements

- For our long-term time frame we will use 50-d and 200-d simple moving averages (SMAs)
- For a stock to pass our technical screen it must meet the following criteria: Uptrending moving averages 50-d SMA above the 200-d SMA and stock price above the 50-d SMA

Common Sense Requirements

- Never buy a stock with a trading volume lower than 500k per day.
- Invest in a minimum of five different stocks in five different industries or sectors where no one security or group will represent more than 20% of your portfolio.
- Allocate equal cash amounts to each segment of our portfolios.
- Portfolio rebalancing should be done at least once a year

Appendix V

Game Plan Summary

Assumptions

The following are assumptions are made for your long-term investment strategy in connection with our wealth-building portfolio:

- You are starting to invest at age 18 with a goal of retiring a millionaire by age 58
- You have little or no money to start but can manage to save $1000 to initiate this journey
- You will save 10% of your gross annual income (earn $10,000; save $1,000.00)
- You will average an annual gross income of $60,000 for the first 20 years and $80,000 for the last 20 years of our 40-year program
- As stated earlier in this book, we will use an annual return of 8%, the lower end of the stock market's historical returns

The preceding and ensuing stats are per-family income earner

3-Step Approach

- Save $1000.00 using work income, gifts and innovative ideas to open your first brokerage account. Make it a "cash" account, not a "margin" account

- $1,000.00 - $25,000.00: Dollar cost average into a broad market index mutual fund (e.g. Charles Schwab broad market index mutual fund).

- Instruct your broker to re-invest all dividends

- $25,000.00 - $1.8 million: Dollar cost average into individual equities using appropriate exit strategies and portfolio rebalancing

- Place trailing stop orders for all stock positions

Summary of Step 3

Here is a summary of our step 3 activity which <u>begins 5 months before reaching our $25,000.00 goal</u>:

- Set up a watch list of 5 stocks in 5 different industries using the FINVIZ screener
- Purchase approximately $1000.00 of each equity at the same time of the month for the next 5 months
- Continue to invest one twelfth of 10% of your gross annual income into your mutual fund account each month

- When the mutual fund account builds up to $5000.00 + transfer $5,000.00 into your stock account making sure enough cash value remains to keep the mutual fund account open
- Continue to purchase $1000.00 of each stock when cash is available
- Increase the number of stocks in your portfolio as its cash value increases
- Use an online discount broker for your journey to financial independence.
- Use a cash account: This is the type of account I recommend as you initiate your investment career.
- Use a 10% trailing stop loss order in our wealth-building portfolio

Management Summary

- Enter a 10% trailing stop loss order (GTC) when originally purchasing the shares

- If the order is executed and shares sold, use the stock screener to select a replacement equity

- Divide the price-per-share of the new stock into the total amount of cash generated from the sale of the original stock to determine the number of new shares to purchase

- Rebalance your portfolio at least once a year

Summary for Covered Call Writing (optional)

Summary of covered call writing in our wealth-building portfolio

- Sell call options that are at least 5% out-of-the-money

- Target 1-month returns of 1-1/2%

- If the strike price is not reached, sell another option the next month

- If the stock price is greater than the strike price as 4PM EST is approached on expiration Friday, roll the option to the next month (example: buy back January $40 call and sell February $40 or $45 call)

- If your shares are sold early (very rare) and there are tax consequences, purchase new shares and identify the new shares as the ones sold (check with your broker)

- If you need cash to roll your options, sell a few shares and retain the majority of your shares

Appendix VI

Master Figure List
of Charts and Graphs

Plans for Alternative Time Frames

SAMPLE 30-Year Plan

Start	$1,000.00
1st 15 years	$8000.00/year
2nd 15 years	$10,000/year
Retirement nest egg	$1,267,515

SAMPLE 20-Year Plan

Start	$5,000.00
1st 10 years	$1500/month
2nd 10 years	$2,000.00/month
Retirement nest egg	$999,760

Figure 51 - Alternate time frames

Glossary

(Includes covered call writing terms not referenced in this book)

Accumulation: Buying of stock by institutional or professional investors over an extended period of time.

Acquisition: When one company purchases the majority interest in the acquired.

Actively Managed Mutual Funds: Shareholders, through a mutual fund manager, buy and sell stocks and bonds, within the fund, in an attempt to *beat the market.*

Advance-Decline Theory: Also called the *Breadth of Market Theory*, this theory states that the market direction can be determined by the number of stocks that have increased compared to those that have decreased in value. It is considered bullish if more shares are advancing than declining.

After hours trading (AHT)- Trading after regular trading hours on the major exchanges.

American Depository Receipt: A negotiable certificate issued by a U.S. bank representing a specified number of shares (or one share) in a foreign stock that is traded on a U.S. exchange. ADRs are denominated in U.S. dollars, with the underlying security held by a U.S. financial institution overseas. ADRs help to reduce administration and duty costs that would otherwise be levied on each transaction.

American Style Options: An option contract that may be exercised at any time between the date of purchase and the expiration date.

Arbitrage: The simultaneous purchase and sale of an asset in order to profit from a difference in the price. It is a trade that profits by exploiting price differences of identical or similar financial instruments, on different markets or in different forms.

Ask: The price a seller is willing to accept for a security. It includes both price and quantity willing to be sold.

Asset allocation- An investment strategy that aims to balance risk and reward by apportioning a portfolio's assets according to an individual's goals, risk tolerance and investment horizon. The main asset classes - equities, fixed-income, real estate and cash and equivalents - have different levels of risk and return, so each will behave differently over time.

Assignment: The receipt of an exercise notice by an option seller that obligates him to sell (in the case of a call) or purchase (in the case of a put) the underlying security at the specified strike price.

At-the-money: An option is at-the-money if the strike price of the option is equal to the market price of the underlying security.

Balance sheet: A financial statement that summarizes a company's assets, liabilities and shareholders' equity at a specific point in time. These three balance sheet segments give investors an idea as to what the company owns and owes, as well as the amount invested by the shareholders. The balance sheet must follow the following formula:

Assets = Liabilities + Shareholders' Equity

Bar Chart: This price chart consists of session high and lows as well as the opening and closing prices. It is also referred to as the Open High Low Close (OHLC) bar.

Basis: Basis is often a moving target. Generally it is what you paid for a stock or option. There are adjustments which may be necessary to report the proper capital gain. These adjustments may include special dividends, stock splits and stock dividends, and some others.

Bearish: Pessimistic investor sentiment that a particular security or market is headed downward.

Beta: This is a measure of the volatility or *systemic risk* (market risk) of a security as compared to the market as a whole.

Bid: An offer made by an investor to buy an equity. It will include price and quantity.

BID/ASK SPREAD: The difference in price between the highest price that a buyer is willing to pay for the option and the lowest price a seller is willing to sell it.

Black-Scholes Option Pricing Model: A model used to calculate the value of an option, by factoring in stock price, strike price and expiration date, risk-free return, and the standard deviation of the stock's return.

Blue chip: A nationally known, well-established and financially sound company. Blue chips generally sell high-quality, widely accepted products and services. Blue chip companies are known to weather downturns and operate profitably in the face of adverse economic conditions, which help to contribute to their long record of stable and reliable growth.

Breakeven: The point at which gains equal losses.

Brokerage account: An arrangement between an investor and a licensed brokerage firm that allows the investor to deposit funds with the firm and place investment orders through the brokerage, which then carries out the transactions on the investor's behalf.

Bullish: Optimistic investor sentiment that a particular equity or market will rise.

Buy down price of stock: Using the intrinsic value of an in-the-money option premium to reduce the cost of the stock purchase.

Buy to close: A term used by many brokerages to represent the closing of a short position in option transactions.

Buy-write order: See net debit order

Calendar Spread- Simultaneously establishing long and short options positions on the same underlying stock with different expiration dates. For example, you buy the December, 2010 $20 call and sell the April, 2010 $20 call on the same equity.

Call option: An option contract giving the owner the right (but not the obligation) to buy a specified amount of an underlying security at a specified price within a specified time.

Candlestick Chart: This chart is created by displaying the high, low, open and close for a security each day over a certain time frame.

Capital Asset : This is pretty much anything you own and use for personal, pleasure or investment purposes. The term includes such tangible assets as a boat, a coin collection, or a piece of real estate. It may also include intangible assets, such as a patent or copyright. The distinction between a capital asset and a non-capital asset is its use. Any capital asset becomes a non-capital asset if it is used in a trade or business, or is "for sale" to customers in a trade or business.

Capital Gain (Loss) : A capital gain or loss is simply the difference between the proceeds of the sale and your cost basis of the asset sold. If you bought a stock for $25 and sold it for $30, you have a capital gain of $5. You can't have a capital gain or loss unless you have a sale of a capital asset. However, a sale of an asset does not necessarily mean you have a capital gain or loss. Why... because every capital gain requires two parts **of the transaction, a sale AND an acquisition, or purchase.**

Cash account: A regular brokerage account in which the customer is required by Regulation T to pay for securities within two days of when a purchase is made.

Cash allocation: Allotting an equivalent amount of cash to each security within a portfolio.

Cash-secured put: When a brokerage company requires us to have the cash in our accounts to purchase the shares we are obligated to buy after selling a put option.

CBOE Volatility Index: (see VIX)

Closed end fund: A closed-end fund is a publicly traded investment company that raises a fixed amount of capital through an initial public offering (IPO). The fund is then structured, listed and traded like a stock on a stock exchange.

Collar (strategy): A protective options strategy that is implemented after a long position in a stock has experienced substantial gains. It is created by purchasing an out of the money put option while simultaneously writing an out of the money call option.

Common stock: A security that represents ownership in a corporation. Holders of common stock exercise control by electing a board of directors and voting on corporate policy. Common stockholders are on the bottom of the priority ladder for ownership structure. In the event of liquidation, common shareholders have rights to a company's assets only after bondholders, preferred shareholders and other debt holders have been paid in full.

Consolidation: *Sideways Pattern (consolidation)* - the horizontal price movement of an equity where the forces of supply and demand are equal. The stock simply cannot establish an uptrend or a downtrend

Contract cycle: The period of time starting with the first trading day after expiration Friday through the end of the following expiration Friday (4 PM EST unless there is an exchange recognized holiday).

Contrary Exercise Notice: If a customer instructs their clearing firm to exercise an "out-of-the-money" option or to abandon an "in-the-money" option, this is a "Contrary Instruction". Contrary Instructions are not allowed in some products.

Convert Dead Money to Cash Profits: An exit strategy wherein an option is bought back and the underlying equity sold. The cash is then used to buy a better performing stock which is used to sell another covered call.

Correlation: This measures the degree to which investments are related.

Cost basis: The original value of an asset. It is used to determine the capital gain, which is equal to the difference between the asset's cost basis and the current market value. Also: the amount of your original investment.

Cost to carry: When money is borrowed from our broker in a margin account, interest is charged and needs to be calculated into our results.

Covered call writing: A strategy in which one sells call options while simultaneously owning the underlying security.

Currency carry trade: A strategy in which an investor sells a certain currency with a relatively low interest rate and uses the funds to purchase a different currency yielding a higher interest rate. A trader using this strategy attempts to capture the difference between the rates, which can often be substantial, depending on the amount of leverage the investor chooses to use.

Custodial account: An account created at a bank, brokerage firm or mutual fund company that is managed by an adult for a minor that is under the age of 18 to 21 (depending on state legislation).

Cyclical stocks: An equity whose price is affected by ups and downs in the overall economy. Cyclical stocks typically relate to companies that sell discretionary items that consumers can afford to buy more of in a bullish economy and will cut back on during a recession. Contrast cyclical stocks with counter-cyclical stocks, which tend to move in the opposite direction from the overall economy, and with consumer staples, which people continue to demand even during a downturn.

Day order: An order to buy or sell a security that automatically expires if not executed on the day the order was placed. A day order is an order that is good for that day only. If it is not filled it will be canceled, and it will not be filled if the limit or stop order price was not met during the trading session.

Defensive stock: A stock that provides a constant dividend and stable earnings regardless of the state of the overall stock market.

Delta: This is the amount an option value will change for every $1 change in the price of a stock. The greater the chance of the strike ending up in-the-money, the higher the delta. Delta values for calls run from 0 to 1.

Derivative: A security whose price is dependent upon or derived from one or more underlying assets. The derivative itself is merely a contract between two or more parties. Its value is determined by fluctuations in the underlying asset. The most common underlying assets include stocks, bonds, commodities, currencies, interest rates and market indexes. Most derivatives are characterized by high leverage.

Diagonal Spread- A long and short options position with different expirations AND strikes. For example, you buy the December, 2010 $20 call and sell the April, 2010 $25 call.

Dilution: A reduction in earnings per share of common stock that occurs through the issuance of additional shares. This is avoided with stock splits by reducing the current market value of a stock by a similar ratio as was the number of shares increased.

Discount broker: See "online discount broker"

Distribution: the selling of stock by large institutions over an extending period of time.

Diversification: A risk management technique that mixes a wide variety of investments within a portfolio. The rationale behind this technique contends that a portfolio of different kinds of investments will, on average, yield higher returns and pose a lower risk than any individual investment found within the portfolio.

Dividend: A distribution of a portion of a company's earnings, decided by the board of directors, to a class of its shareholders.

Dollar cost averaging: The technique of buying a fixed dollar amount of a particular investment on a regular schedule, regardless of the share price. More shares are purchased when prices are low, and fewer shares are bought when prices are high.

Downside protection: The intrinsic value portion of an in-the-money call option premium divided by the original cost basis. It is the percentage of your investment that can be lost without affecting the option return on your investment. The formula is as follows:

Intrinsic Value of option premium

_____ = % of downside protection

Original Cost of stock

Down trending Stock: A stock with a declining share price showing lower highs and lower lows.

The Dow Theory: This theory states that the market is in an upward trend if one of the averages (industrial or transportation) advances above a previous significant high and is accompanied by a similar advance in the other. A major trend is identified only when BOTH the Dow Industrial and Dow Transportation Averages reach a new high or a new low. Without this confirmation, the market will return to its previous trading pattern.

Earnings estimate: An analyst's estimate for a company's future quarterly or annual earnings.

Earnings guidance: Information that a company provides as an indication or estimate of their future earnings.

Earnings per share: The portion of a company's profit allocated to each outstanding share of common stock. Earnings per share serves as an indicator of a company's profitability.

Calculated as:

$$= \frac{\text{Net Income - Dividends on Preferred Stock}}{\text{Average Outstanding Shares}}$$

Earnings report: A quarterly filing made by public companies to report their performance. Included in these reports are items such as net income, earnings per share, earnings from continuing operations, and net sales. These reports follow the end of each quarter. Most companies file in January, April, July, and October.

Earnings surprise: When the earnings reported in a companies quarterly or annual report are above or below analysts' earnings estimates.

Efficient frontier: A line created from the risk-reward graph, comprised of optimal portfolios.

Elite Calculator: Expanded version of the basic Ellman Calculator (ESOC) which includes an *unwind tab* and a *Schedule D*.

Ellman Calculator- See ESOC.

Emerging growth stock: A company in a line of business formed around a new product or idea that is in the early stages of development. An emerging company typically is often centered around a new technology.

ESOC: Ellman System Option Calculator which is an excel calculator used to compute option returns specifically for Alan Ellman's *Cashing In On Covered Calls* system.

ETFs: See exchange traded funds.

Exchange traded funds: A security that tracks an index, a commodity, or a basket of assets like an index fund, but trades like a stock on an exchange, thus experiencing price changes throughout the day as it is bought and sold. These securities provide the diversification of an index fund.

Exercise: When you exercise your stock option, you "trade in" your options for the actual stock.

European Style Option: An option contract that can only be exercised on the expiration date.

Execution (of a trade): The completion of a buy or sell stock order.

Exercise by exception: A procedure used by OCC as an operational convenience for its clearing members. Under these proceedings, a clearing member is deeming to have tendered exercise notices for options that are in-the-money by threshold amounts, unless specifically instructed not to do so. This procedure protects the owner from losing the intrinsic value of the option because of failure to exercise. Unless instructed not to do so, all expiring equity options that are held in customer accounts will be exercised if they are in the money by a specified amount.

Exit strategy: A plan in which a trader intends to get out of an investment position made in the past. It is a way of *cashing out* or *closing out a position.*

Expected Return: Possible return on a portfolio in different market conditions (bullish, bearish and neutral) weighted by the likelihood that the return will occur.

Expense ratio: A measure of what it costs an investment company to operate a mutual fund. It is determined through an annual calculation, where a fund's operating expenses are

256

divided by the average dollar value of its managed assets Operating expenses are taken out of a fund's assets and lower the return to a fund's investors. Some funds have a marketing cost referred to as a 12b-1 fee, which would also be included in operating expenses. It is interesting that a fund's trading activity - the buying and selling of stock - is NOT included in the calculation of expense ratio.

Expiration date: The last day (in the case of an American- style) or the only day (in the case of European-style) on which an option may be exercised. For stock option, this date is the third Friday of the expiration month. If Friday is a holiday, the last trading day is the preceding Thursday.

Exponential moving average or EMA: A type of moving average that is similar to a simple moving average, except that more weight is given to the most recent data. It reacts faster to recent price changes than does a simple moving average. The 12- and 26-day EMA's are the most popular short-term averages, and they are used to create indicators like the MACD.

Fair value: Refers to the relationship between the futures contract on a market index like the S&P 500 and the actual value of the index. If the futures are above fair value then traders are betting the market index will go higher, the opposite is true if futures are below fair value.

First call: A company that gathers research notes and earnings estimates from brokerage analysts and forms a consensus estimate. The estimate is compared to the actual earnings reports, and then the difference between the two is the earnings surprise. The other major player in this estimate game is **Zachs.**

Full service broker: A broker that provides a large variety of services to its clients, including research and advice, retirement planning, tax tips, and more. Commissions at full-service brokerages are much higher than those at discount brokers.

Fundamental analysis: A method of analyzing the prospects of a security by observing the accepted accounting measures such as earnings, sales, and assets and so on.

Gamma: The rate of change for delta with respect to the price of the underlying security. It is an estimate of how much the delta of an option changes when the price of the stock moves $1.

Gap: A gap is a break between prices on a chart that occurs when the price of a stock makes a sharp move up or down with no trading occurring in between.

Globalization: The tendency of investment funds and businesses to move beyond domestic and national markets to other markets around the globe, thereby increasing the interconnectedness of different markets. It has had the effect of increasing international trade and cultural exchange.

Greeks: A mathematical means of estimating the risk of stock options. Delta measures the change in the option price due to a change in the stock price, gamma measures the change in the option delta due to a change in the stock price, theta measures the change in the option price due to time passing, vega measures the change in the option price due to volatility changing, and rho measures the change in the option price due to a change in interest rates.

Growth stock: Shares in a company whose earnings are expected to grow at an above-average rate relative to the market.

GTC order: An order to buy or sell a security at a set price that is active until the investor decides to cancel it or the trade is executed. If an order does not have a "good-'til-canceled" instruction then the order will expire at the end of the trading day the order was placed. In most cases, GTC orders are canceled by brokerage firms after 30-90 days.

Historical volatility: This is the actual price fluctuation as observed over a period of time.

Hit a Double: An exit strategy wherein an option is bought back and then resold at a higher premium in the same contract period.

Hit a Triple: An exit strategy wherein an option is bought back and resold twice in the same contract period.

Horizontal Spread- A spread where both options have the same strike price as in the above example but different expiration dates. *The terms calendar and horizontal spreads are interchangeable.*

Hypothecation agreement: When a person pledges securities in a margin account used as collateral for money loaned from a brokerage.

IBD 100: The Investor's Business Daily 100 is a computer-generated ranking of the leading companies trading in America. Rankings are based on a combination of each company's profit growth; IBD's Composite Rating, which includes key measures such as return on equity, sales growth and profit margins; and relative price strength in the past 12 months.

Implied Volatility- This is a forecast of the underlying stock's volatility as implied by the option's price in the marketplace.

Income statement: A financial statement that measures a company's financial performance over a specific accounting period. Financial performance is assessed by giving a summary of how the business incurs its revenues and expenses through both operating and non-operating activities. It also shows the net profit or loss incurred over a specific accounting period, typically over a fiscal quarter or year. Also known as the "profit and loss statement"

Income stock: Stocks that have lower levels of volatility than the overall stock market and offer higher-than-market dividend yields. Income stocks may have limited future growth options, thereby requiring a lower level of ongoing capital investment. The excess cash flow from profits can therefore be directed back toward investors on a regular basis. They are most commonly found as companies operating within real estate, energy sectors, utilities, natural resources and financial institutions.

Index fund: A type of mutual fund with a portfolio constructed to mirror, or track, the components of a market index such as the S&P 500 Index. An index mutual fund is said to provide broad market exposure, low operating expenses and low portfolio turnover. *Indexing* is a passive form of fund management that has been successful in out-performing most actively managed mutual funds.

Index futures: A futures contract on a stock or financial index. For each index there may be a different multiple for determining the price of the futures contract.

Industry: A classification that refers to a group of companies that are related in terms of their primary business activities. In modern economies, there are dozens of different industry classifications, which are typically grouped into larger categories called sectors.

Internal rate of return: IRR is a way to analyze an investment considering the time value of money. It basically calculates the interest rate which is the equivalent of the dollar amount your investment will return

In-the-money: A term describing any option that has *intrinsic value*. A call option is in-the-money if the underlying security is higher than the strike price of the call.

Intrinsic value: The value of an option if it were to expire immediately with the underlying stock at its current price; the amount by which the stock is in-the-money. For call options, this is the positive difference between the stock price and the strike price.

Investing: The act of committing money to an endeavor (a business, project, real estate, stock market etc.) with the expectation of generating an additional income or profit.

Investor Fear Gauge: See VIX.

IPO (initial public offering): The first sale of stock by a private company to the public.

Joint account: A brokerage account that is shared between two or more individuals. Joint accounts are most likely to be used between relatives, couples or business partners who have a level of familiarity and trust for each other, as this type of account typically allows anyone named on the account to access funds within it.

Joint tenants and the right of survivorship (JTWROS): A type of brokerage account which is owned by at least two people, where all tenants have an equal right to the account's assets and are afforded survivorship rights in the event of the death of another account holder.

Joint tenants in common (JTIC): A type of brokerage account which is owned by at least two people with no rights of survivorship afforded to any of the account holders.

Key economic indicator: Macroeconomic data that is used by investors to interpret current or future investment possibilities and judge the overall health of an economy. These are specific pieces of data released by the government and non-profit organizations. These include:

- The Consumer Price Index (CPI)
- Gross Domestic Product (GDP)
- Unemployment statistics
- The price of crude oil

Laddering: This is an investment technique whereby investors purchase multiple financial products with different maturity dates. I have borrowed this term and used it to describe a covered call t5echnique where different strike prices are used for the same equity.

262

Lagging indicator: A technical indicator that trails the price action of an underlying asset. It is used by traders to generate transaction signals or to confirm the strength of a given trend. Since these indicators lag the price of the asset, a significant move will generally occur before the indicator is able to provide a signal. It confirms long-term trends but does not predict them.

Large cap: An abbreviation for the term *large market capitalization.* Market capitalization is calculated by multiplying the number of a company's outstanding shares by its stock price per share. The expression *large cap* is used by the investment community as an indicator of a company's size. A large cap stock has a market-capitalization dollar value of over 10 billion.

LEAPS- Long-Term Equity Anticipation Securities. These are option contracts with expiration dates longer than one year. Only the more heavily traded stocks and ETFs have these types of options associated with them.

Legging in: A way of executing a covered call trade wherein we first buy the stock and, once owned, sell the corresponding call option.

Limit Order: An order placed by a brokerage to buy or sell a specified number of shares at a specific price or better. The length of time an order remains outstanding can also be specified.

Line Chart: This is a very basic chart created by connecting a series of closing prices of a particular security with a line.

Liquidity: The degree to which an asset or security can be bought or sold in the market without affecting the asset's price.

Long (position): The buying of a security, such as a stock or options contract, with the expectation that the asset will rise in value.

MACD (Moving average convergence divergence): A trend-following momentum indicator that shows the relationship between two moving averages of prices. The MACD is calculated by subtracting the 26-day exponential moving average (EMA) from the 12-day EMA. A 9-day EMA of the MACD, called the *signal line,* is then plotted on top of the MACD, functioning as a trigger for buy and sell signals.

MACD Histogram: A common technical indicator that illustrates the difference between the MACD and the trigger line. This difference is then plotted on a chart in the form of a histogram to make it easy for a trader to determine a specific asset's momentum.

Margin account: This is a brokerage account where the client has the ability to borrow money from the broker to purchase securities. This loan is then collateralized by the cash and securities in that specific account.

Margin call: When the value of the securities in a margin account drop to a certain level, the investor will be required to put additional cash in the account or sell certain securities

Market capitalization: The total dollar market value of all of a company's outstanding shares. It is calculated by multiplying a company's shares outstanding by the current market price of one share. The investment community uses this figure to determine a company's size, as opposed to sales or total asset figures. Also referred to as *market cap.*

Market consensus: The average earnings estimates made by brokers and security analysts. Also known as *earnings expectations*.

Market Order: An order to buy or sell a stock at the current best available price.

Market psychology: The overall sentiment or feeling that the market is experiencing at any particular time. Greed, fear, expectations and circumstances are all factors that contribute to the group's overall investing mentality or sentiment.

Market sector: An industry or market sharing common characteristics. Investors use sectors to place stocks and other investments into categories like technology, health care, energy, utilities and telecommunications. Each sector has unique characteristics and a different risk profile.

Market Tone: The feeling of a market (general psychology) as demonstrated by the price activity of stocks. We use the VIX and S&P 500 chart patterns to help assess this sentiment.

Married put: When the protective put is purchased on the same day as the stock, it is referred to as a *married put* for tax purposes.

Mergers: A general term used to refer to the consolidation of companies. It is a combination of two companies to form a new company.

Modern portfolio theory: A portfolio optimization methodology that utilizes the mean variance of investment returns. It uses the standard deviation of all returns as a measure of risk.

Momentum indicator: Designed to track momentum in the price of a security to help identify the enthusiasm of buyers and sellers involved in the price trend development. Some indicators compare the closing price with some historical price so many periods before; others construct trend lines like the *MACD*. Others, like *Stochastics,* is a ratio using the high, low, and close values on various days.

Momentum Oscillator: A technical analysis tool that is banded between two extreme values and built with the results from a trend indicator for discovering short-term overbought or oversold conditions. As the value of the oscillator approaches the upper extreme value the asset is deemed to be overbought, and as it approaches the lower extreme it is deemed to be oversold. This oscillator is most advantageous when a stock price is in a trading range (sideways). An example is the *stochastic oscillator*

Money market securities: The securities market dealing in short-term debt and monetary instruments. These forms of debt mature in less than one year and are quite liquid. Treasury bills make up the bulk of the money market instruments. These securities are relatively risk-free.

Moving average: An indicator frequently used in technical analysis showing the average value of a securities price over a set period. Moving averages are generally used to measure momentum and define areas of possible support and resistance.

Multiple Tab of the ESOC: Compare returns, upside potential, and downside protection for many stocks, all on the same page.

Mutual fund: An investment vehicle that is made up of a pool of funds collected from many investors for the purpose of investing in securities such as stocks, bonds, money market instruments and similar assets. Mutual funds are operated by money managers, who invest the fund's capital and attempt to produce capital gains and income for the fund's investors. A mutual fund's portfolio is structured and maintained to match the investment objectives stated in its prospectus.

Nasdaq 100 index: An index composed of the 100 largest, most actively traded U.S. companies listed on the Nasdaq stock exchange. This index includes companies from a broad range of industries with the exception of those that operate in the financial industry, such as banks and investment companies.

NAV (net asset value): A mutual fund's price per share or exchange-traded fund's (ETF) per-share value. In both cases, the per-share dollar amount of the fund is calculated by dividing the total value of all the securities in its portfolio, less any liabilities, by the number of fund shares outstanding.

Net debit order: This is where you buy the stock and sell the option at the exact same time, not for specific corresponding prices but for a *limit net debit*. Also called a *buy-write*.

Non Standard Options: These are options that don't have the standard terms of an options contract, namely 100 shares as the underlying asset.

OCO order (one cancels other): A pair of orders stipulating that if one order is executed, then the other order is automatically canceled. A one-cancels-the-other order (OCO) combines a stop order with a limit order on an automated trading platform. When either the stop or limit level is reached and the order executed, the other order will be automatically canceled.

Odd Lot Theory: This theory is based on the assumption that the small investor is always wrong. Since these investors usually buy and sell in odd-lot amounts (less than 100 shares) and have low risk-tolerance (the theory continues), they tend to buy high and sell low. A bullish signal is when odd-lot sell orders increase relative to odd-lot buy orders.

OHLC (bar) chart: Short for *Open High, Low Close chart.* This type of chart is used to spot trends and view stock movements, particularly on a short term basis.

Online Discount Broker: A stockbroker who carries out buy and sell orders online, at reduced commissions, but provides no investment advice.

Open end fund: A type of mutual fund that does not have restrictions on the amount of shares the fund will issue. If demand is high enough, the fund will continue to issue shares no matter how many investors there are. Open-end funds also buy back shares when investors wish to sell. The majority of mutual funds are open-end.

Open interest- The open interest of an option contract is the number of outstanding options of that type which currently have not been closed out or exercised

Option: A contract that gives the owner the right, if exercised, to buy or sell a security or basket of securities (index) at a specific price within a specific time limit. Stock option contracts are generally for the right to buy or sell 100 shares of the underlying stock.

Option account: An account opened with an options or securities firm that permits a customer to trade options. The customer opening an option account must have margin and sign an options agreement prior to trading.

Option chain: A way of quoting option prices through a list of all the options for a given security. For each underlying security, the option chain tells investors the various strike prices, expiration dates, and whether they are calls or puts.

Options contract: Represents 100 shares in the underlying stock. Information included consists of the underlying security, type of option (call or put), expiration month, strike price and premium.

Option premium: The price at which the contract trades. It is the price paid by the buyer to the .writer, or seller, of the option. In return the writer of the call option is obligated to deliver the underlying security to an option buyer if the call is exercised or buy the underlying security if the put is exercised. The writer keeps the premium whether or not the option is exercised.

OTO order (one triggers other): A one triggers the other orders involves two orders—a primary order and a secondary order. The primary order may be a live order in the marketplace. The secondary order, held in a separate order file, is not. If the primary order executes in full, the secondary order is released to the marketplace and becomes live.

Out-of-the-money: A call option is out-of-the-money if the strike price is greater than market value of the underlying security.

Over-the-counter option (OTC): An option traded off-exchange, as opposed to a *listed* stock option. The OTC option has a direct link between buyer and seller, has no secondary market, and has no standardization of strike prices and expiration dates. This securities market is not geographically centralized like the trading floor of the NYSE. Trading takes place through a telephone and computer network.

Overbought: A technical condition that occurs when prices are considered too high and susceptible to decline. Overbought conditions can be classified by analyzing the chart pattern or with indicators such as the Stochastic Oscillator. Generally, a security is considered overbought when the Stochastic Oscillator exceeds 80. Overbought is not the same as being *bearish. It simply infers that the stock has risen too far too fast and might be due for a pullback.*

Oversold: A technical condition that occurs when prices are considered too low and ripe for a surge. Oversold conditions can be classified by analyzing the chart pattern or with indicators such as the Stochastic Oscillator. Generally, a security is considered oversold if the Stochastic Oscillator is less than 20. Oversold is not the same as being *bullish. It merely infers that the security has fallen too far too fast and may be due for a reaction rally.*

Painting the tape: An illegal action by a group of market manipulators buying and/or selling a security among themselves to create artificial trading activity, which, when reported on the ticker tape, attracts unsuspecting investors as they perceive unusual volume.

Paper trade: A hypothetical trade that does not involve any monetary transactions. It is a risk-free way to learn the ins and outs of the market.

Passive management (of mutual funds): An investment strategy that mirrors a market index and does not attempt to beat the market.

PE Ratio: P/E Ratio or Price-Earnings Ratio is a valuation ratio that compares the price of a stock to it's per share earnings.

PEG Ratio: PEG = PE Ratio/Annual EPS Growth

PEGY Ratio: = PE Ratio/ Expected Earnings Growth + Dividend Yield

Pinning the strike: This is when puts and calls are near the money on expiration Friday. There is a tendency called *pinning the strike* for the stock to move to the strike price or slightly beyond.

Portfolio management: The art and science of making decisions about investment mix and policy, matching investments to objectives, asset allocation, and balancing risk versus performance. *It requires organized lists of accurate information.*

Portfolio overwriting: This is where a call option is sold on a stock already part of an existing portfolio. That option is selected in a manner such that the option is NOT expected to be exercised as every effort is made to retain the equity.

Portfolio rebalancing: The process of realigning the weightings of one's portfolio of assets. Rebalancing involves periodically buying or selling assets in your portfolio to maintain your original desired level of asset allocation.

Preferred stock: A class of ownership in a corporation that has a higher claim on the assets and earnings than common stock. Preferred stock generally have dividends that must be paid out before dividends to common stockholders and the shares usually do not have voting rights.

Premium report: The weekly stock screen and watch list published by the Blue Collar Investor Corp. This is a screen specific for candidates geared to writing 1-month covered calls.

Price-to-book ratio (P/B): A ratio used to compare a stock's market value to its book value. It is calculated by dividing the current closing price of the stock by the latest quarter's book value per share. It is also known as the "price-equity ratio".

Calculated as:

$$P/B\,Ratio = \frac{Stock\,Price}{Total\,Assets - Intangible\,Assets\,and\,Liabilities}$$

Protective put: A put option purchased for a stock that is already owned by the owner of the option. A *protective put* defends against a decrease in the share price of the underlying security

Price bar: see *OHLC.*

Protective put: A put option purchased for a stock that is already owned by the owner of the option. A *protective put*

defends against a decrease in the share price of the underlying security.

Pump and dump scam: A scheme that attempts to boost the price of a stock through recommendations based on false, misleading or greatly exaggerated statements. The perpetrators of this scheme, who already have an established position in the company's stock, sell their positions after the hype has led to a higher share price. This practice is illegal based on securities law and can lead to heavy fines.

Put option: An option contract that gives the holder the right, but not the obligation, to sell the underlying security at a specified price for a certain fixed period of time.

QQQ: This is the ticker symbol for the Nasdaq 100 Trust, which is an exchange traded fund (ETF) that trades on the Nasdaq. It offers broad exposure to the tech sector by tracking the Nasdaq 100 index, which consists of the 100 largest non-financial stocks on the Nasdaq.

Ratio valuation: A form of fundamental analysis that looks to compare the valuation of one security to another, to a group of securities or within its own historical context. Valuation analysis is done to evaluate the potential merits of an investment or to objectively assess the value of a company. For equities, the most common valuation metric to use is the P/E ratio, although other valuation metrics include: Price/Earnings, Price/Book, Price/Sales among others.

Resistance: The price level at which there is a large enough supply of a stock available to cause a halt in the upward trend and turn the trend down. Resistance levels indicate the price at which most investors feel that the prices will move lower.

Return on equity (ROE): The amount of net income returned as a percentage of shareholders equity. Return on equity measures a corporation's profitability by revealing how much profit a company generates with the money shareholders have invested. ROE is expressed as a percentage and calculated as:

Return on Equity = Net Income/Shareholder's Equity

Net income is for the full fiscal year (before dividends paid to common stock holders but after dividends to preferred stock.) Shareholder's equity does not include preferred shares.

Reverse stock split: A decrease in the number of a corporation's shares outstanding that increases the par value of its stock or its earnings per share. The market value of the total number of shares (market capitalization) remains the same.

Rho: Not considered a major Greek, measures the change in the option price due to a change in interest rates.

Risk: The chance that an investment's actual return will be different than expected. Risk includes the possibility of losing some or all of the original investment.

Risk-reward profile: A risk reward profile is a chart of the theoretical maximum profit or loss a particular investment can have in your portfolios.

Rolling down: Closing out options at one strike price and simultaneously opening another at a lower strike price.

Rolling out (forward): Closing out of an option contract at a near-term expiration date and opening a same strike option contract at a later date.

Rolling up: Close out options at a lower strike and open options at a higher strike.

ROO (return on option): The percent profit realized from the sale of a covered call option based on the cost basis of the underlying stock. If an in-the-money option was sold, the intrinsic value is deducted from the option premium before calculating the return.

Rule of 72: A rule stating that in order to find the number of years required to double your money at a given interest rate; you divide the compound return into 72. The result is the approximate number of years that it will take for your investment to double.

S&P 500 (Standard and Poor's 500): An index consisting of 500 stocks chosen for market size, liquidity, and industry grouping, among other factors. It is designed to be a leading indicator of U.S. equities and is meant to reflect the risk/return characteristics of the large-cap universe.

Sarbanes-Oxley Act of 2002 (SOX): An act passed by the U.S. Congress to protect investors from the possibility of fraudulent accounting activities by corporations. It includes the establishment of a *Public Company Accounting Oversight Board* where public companies must now be registered.

Securities and Exchange Commission (SEC): A government commission, created by Congress, established to regulate the securities markets and protect investors. It also monitors the corporate takeovers in the U.S. The SEC is composed of five commissions appointed by the U.S. President and approved by the Senate. The statutes administered by the SEC are designed to promote full public disclosure and to protect the investing public against fraudulent and manipulative practices in the securities markets. Generally, most issues of securities offered in interstate commerce, through the mail or on the internet, must be registered with the SEC.

Sell to open: A phrase used by many brokerages on the street to represent the opening of a short position in option transactions.

Short (or short position): The sale (also known as *writing*) of an options contract or a stock to open a position.

Short sale: Short sale is the sale of a stock not owned by the seller. It is borrowed from the broker and eventually must be replaced. The seller anticipates a decline in equity value and realizes a profit by covering (buying back) the short sale at a lower price in the future.

Show or Fill Rule: This regulation requires the market makers to show or publish any order that improves the current bid or ask prices unless it is filled.

Short Interest Theory: This theory states that a larger short interest is the predecessor of an increase in the price of a stock.

Sideways Pattern (consolidation) – This is the horizontal price movement of an equity where the forces of supply and demand are equal. The stock simply cannot establish an uptrend or a downtrend.

Simple moving average (SMA): A moving average that gives equal weight to each day's price data.

Single Tab of the ESOC: Allows you to evaluate returns from different strikes for the same stock.

Standard Deviation: This is a statistical measurement that sheds light on historical volatility.

Stochastic Oscillator: A momentum indicator that measures the price of a security relative to the high/low range over a set period of time. The indicator oscillates between 0 and 100. Readings below 20 are considered oversold. Readings above 80 are considered overbought.

StockScouter Rating: MSN Monet Central's rating of stocks from 1 to 10, with 10 being the best. It uses a system of advanced mathematics to determine a stock's expected risk and return.

Stock split: A change in the number of shares outstanding (in circulation). The number of shares is adjusted by the split ratio, e.g. 2 to 1. In this case, 1000 shares splits to 2000 shares but the opening price and current price are cut in half. The overall effect is to maintain the same cost and current value of an investment while increasing the number of shares and lowering the per share price. This makes it easier for small investors to own the stock in round lots.

Stop loss order: This is an order placed with your broker to sell a security when it reaches a certain price.

Stop Order: This is an order to buy or sell a security when its price surpasses a specific price called the *stop price*. At that point the stop order becomes a *market order*.

Stop Limit Order: This is a combination of a *stop order* and a *limit order*. Once activated, it becomes a limit order which means that it can only be executed at a specific price or better.

Street expectation: The average earnings estimates made by brokers and security analysts.

Strike price: The stated price per share for which the underlying security may be purchased (in the case of a call) or sold (in the case of a put) by the option holder upon exercise of the option contract.

Support: A price level at which there is sufficient demand for a stock to cause a halt in a downward trend and turn the trend up. Support levels indicate the price at which most investors feel that prices will move higher.

Technical analysis: The method of predicting future stock price movements based on observation of historical stock price movements.

Theoretical Value: The hypothetical value of an option as calculated by a mathematical model such as the *Black-Scholes Option Pricing Model.*

Theta: Theta is an estimate of how much the theoretical value of an option declines when there is a *passage of one day* while there is no change in the stock value or volatility. Theta is expressed as a negative number since the passage of time will decrease time value.

Ticker symbol: An arrangement of characters (usually letters) representing a particular security listed on an exchange. Every listed security has a unique ticker symbol, facilitating the trade orders that flow through the financial markets every day.

Time decay: A term used to describe how the theoretical value of an option *erodes* or reduces with the passage of time.

Time value: The portion of the option premium that is attributable to the amount of time remaining until the expiration of the option contract. Time value is whatever value the option has in addition to its intrinsic value.

Trading: Trading is a more active, short-term strategy than investing. Buying and selling frequently to take profits rather than accumulate long term growth.

Trading range: The spread between the high and low prices traded during a period of time.

Trailing stop loss order: A stop-loss order set at a percentage level below the market price - for a long position. The trailing stop price is adjusted as the price fluctuates. The trailing stop order can be placed as a trailing stop limit order, or a trailing stop market order.

Treasury note (one of the *treasuries*): A marketable, U.S. government debt security with a fixed interest rate and a maturity between one and ten years. T-notes can be bought either directly from the U.S. Government or through a bank.

Trend analysis: An aspect of technical analysis that tries to predict the future movement of a stock based on past data. It is based on the idea that what has happened in the past gives traders an idea of what will happen in the future. The concept is that moving with trends will lead to profits for the investor.

Trigger line / signal: Usually an exponential or simple moving average of a technical indicator which serves as a frame of reference for positive and negative divergences. For example, if the MACD indicator moves above its moving average, a bullish signal is produced.

Unit investment trust (UIT): An investment company that offers a fixed, unmanaged portfolio, generally of stocks and bonds, as redeemable "units" to investors for a specific period of time. It is designed to provide capital appreciation and/or dividend income. Unit investment trusts are one of three types of investment companies; the other two are mutual funds and closed-end funds.

Upside potential: Additional % of profit, as it relates to the underlying stock cost basis that can be realized if the stock price reaches the strike price at expiration. It applies to out-of-the-money strike prices.

Uptrending Stock: This is a stock increasing in price with higher highs and higher lows.

Vega: Vega is the only "Greek" not represented by a real Greek letter. It is the amount that the price of an option changes compared to a 1% change in volatility.

Velocity (of money): A term used to describe the rate at which money is exchanged from one transaction to another.

VIX- CBOE Volatility Index: Demonstrates the market's expectation of 30-day volatility. It measures market risk and is often referred to as the *investor fear gauge*.

Volatility: This is the fluctuation, not direction, of a stock price movement. It represents the deviation of day to day price changes. It measures the speed and magnitude at which the underlying equity's price changes.

Volume: The number of trades in a security over a period of time. On a chart, volume is usually represented as a histogram (vertical bars) below the price chart. The NYSE and Nasdaq measure volume differently. For every buyer, there is a seller: 100 shares bought = 100 shares sold. The NYSE would count this as 100 shares of volume. However, the Nasdaq would count each side of the trade and as 200 shares volume.

Volume confirmation: Using the volume indicator indicator or chart pattern to provide evidence that the initial trading alert in question is indicative of an actual trading opportunity. Traders look to other technical indicators to confirm their expected prediction so that they can have as many technical factors working in their favor as possible. This increases the probability of making a highly successful trade.

Volume divergence: When the price of a stock and the volume indicator move in opposite directions. In technical analysis, traders make transaction decisions by identifying situations of divergence, where the price of a stock and an indicator such as volume are moving in opposite directions. Divergence is considered either positive or negative, both of which are signals of major shifts in the direction of the price. Positive divergence occurs when the price of a security makes a new low while the indicator starts to climb upward. Negative divergence happens when the price of the security makes a new high, but the indicator fails to do the same and instead closes lower than the previous high.

Volume surge: An increase in the daily trading volume of an equity equal to at least 1.5 times its normal trading volume.

Wash Sale: A wash sale loss is not deductible. A wash sale occurs when you sell a stock for a loss and, within 30 days before or after the trade, buy the same stock, or substantially the same stock. This means that if you sell a stock at $35 for a loss, and buy a $35 call option, you have a wash sale and cannot deduct the loss on the stock.

Watch list: A list of securities that are in consideration for investment buy/sell decisions.

What Now Tab of the ESOC: Calculates the returns for a package transaction where an option is bought back and another is sold.

Whisper number: The unofficial and unpublished earnings per share (EPS) forecasts that circulate among professionals on Wall Street. They were generally reserved for the favored (wealthy) clients of a brokerage.

Wilshire 5000 Total Stock Market Index: A market capitalization-weighted index composed of more than 6700 publicly traded companies. These companies must be headquartered in the U.S. and actively traded on an American stock exchange.

Yen carry trade: A strategy in which an investor sells the Japanese currency (yen) with a relatively low interest rate and uses the funds to purchase a different currency (dollar) yielding a higher interest rate. A trader using this strategy attempts to capture the difference between the rates-which can often be substantial, depending on the amount of leverage the investor chooses to use.

Yield curve: A line that plots the interest rates, at a set point in time, of bonds having equal credit quality, but differing maturity dates. The most frequently reported yield curve compares the three-month, two-year, five-year and 30-year U.S. Treasury debt. This yield curve is used as a benchmark for other debt in the market, such as mortgage rates or bank lending rates. The curve is also used to predict changes in economic output and growth.

About the Author

Dr. Alan Ellman, author of best-selling *Cashing in on Covered Calls, Exit Strategies for Covered Call Writing and* Alan Ellman's *Encyclopedia for Covered Call Writing* has been devoting more and more of his time to teaching retail investors (Blue Collar Investors) the art and science of investing with stocks and options. He is also a recently retired general Dentist from the state of New York, a certified personal fitness trainer and a licensed Real Estate Salesperson. Dr. Ellman has also successfully completed his Series 65 certification as an Investment Advisor.

As a real estate investor, Alan owns both commercial and residential properties in Texas, Pennsylvania, New York and Florida. He has frequently been invited to speak about his successful investment properties in front of large groups of real estate investors.

In the past six years, Alan has been increasing the time he spends educating investors in the arena of stock options and specifically covered call options. He writes a weekly journal article that is published on his website and responds to email questions from all over the world. Alan has also been interviewed on numerous financial radio programs and has hosted dozens of seminars on this investment strategy. Alan is a national speaker for *The Money Show* and the *American Association of Individual Investors*. His goal is for you to achieve financial independence through education, motivation and due-diligence. To learn how to best accomplish these goals and become CEO of your own money visit his web site at:

www.thebluecollarinvestor.com

Index

Numerics

A-Z

288